Silent
Voices

Written by Jonathon Toy

Silent Voices

Silent Voices

In association with

Silent Voices

Silent Voices

Published in London by Peaches Publications, 2016.
www.peachespublications.weebly.com

The moral right of the author has been asserted.

Characters mentioned are an amalgamation of different people and not based on one single person. The stories are true to the author's recollection. Some people's names have been changed for confidentially reasons.

British Library Cataloguing in Publication Data: A catalogue record for this book is available from the British Library.

ISBN: 978-1-326-62785-0

Front and back cover design: Oscar Wilson-Toy.

Proof read and critique: Freya Towli.

Copy editor: Karen Cannon.

Typesetter and Editor: Winsome Duncan.

Table of Contents

Simon Harding
Senior Lecturer, Middlesex University

This work is therefore undertaken in the best tradition of ethnography: a deep immersion in this world and desire to foreground the voices of those who live in it.

It has no pretensions to situate the work in gang theory. It simply does not need to. In fact, to do so would dampen the raw emotion so evocatively captured and render the experiences no more than a case study.

Sheldon Thomas
Former gang leader and Gangs Consultant at Gangsline

A very insightful approach with each chapter making for compelling read, giving us the reader a unique insight into gang lifestyle seen from a different prospective. Some researchers often use poverty, unemployment, deprivation as the core reasons why some turn to gangs and crime. This book must be read if you want to have some understanding on gangs.

Commander John Sutherland
Metropolitan Police Service

Before we can begin to resolve the problems we're faced with, we need to have a better conversation about youth violence - starting with the development of a much a better understanding of what it is that we're faced with. This book is an important contribution to that conversation

Dedication

———————————

To Corey and his family, I have never forgotten you and
your memory has inspired me to make a difference.

Acknowledgements

There are many people who have contributed to this book. Firstly can I thank Freya Towli who supported me in proof reading and was my most valued critical friend throughout. To Karen Cannon who helped editing and making sense of my often clumsy writing. To the friends at the Central Criminal Justice Court, who let me peer into their insightful world. To the police investigators and members of the Hamrow Team in Southwark, who sacrifice so much of their lives to keep us safe.

I would like to pay a particular tribute to Sheldon Thomas from Gangs Line and Gwenton Sloley both of whom have shared an amazing journey with me over the last decade.

I would like to make a specific acknowledgement to my dear friend Grace Idowu, who was one of the inspirations behind this book. Grace we love you and thank you for sharing your love of David.

I would like to thank all of the people who allowed me to share your stories. I won't name you for reasons far too obvious, but you know who you are and your words are written large on these pages.

Finally, I would like to thank my beautiful family, who have endured nearly two decades of me putting others first. I could promise to change but, enough promises have been broken already. Instead, can say how much I love you, thank for your patience and your understanding.

I would also like to say sorry; sorry to Sunday, Samuel, Michael, Femi, Dogan, Levan, Ola, Osman, David, Lyle and all of the others who are no longer with us. I am sorry you are not here, fulfilling your potential, making your families proud and enriching their lives. You have all made a difference and are a constant reminder that we all need to stand shoulder to shoulder to stop violence.

Foreword

by John Pitts,
Vauxhall Professor of Socio-legal Studies,
University of Bedfordshire

Over the past decade research into 'group offending' in English cities has proliferated. Criminologists, sociologists and psychologists have argued vociferously about whether these groups can be defined as 'street gangs' and, if so, how and why young people become involved with them; who these young people are; what they do when they are involved and why most of them eventually desist from gang involvement. What few of these studies reveal, however, is the brutality of the 'street worlds' that these young people inhabit or the pathos of their lives.

Silent Voices is a shocking book. So shocking that at times one turns away from the page. And this is because the people involved with the violent gang murder at the heart of the book, the perpetrators, their associates, the victim's friends and family, the teacher; the investigating police officer; the trial judge and the surgeon who struggled for a week to save the victims life, all speak, as it were, 'directly to camera'.

They tell us who they are and something of their life histories. In this way we gradually come to see why they see this murder as they do, But, when the young people speak, we are forced to confront the ways that early experiences of war, gang-related brutality, acute domestic violence, parental sexual abuse, profound neglect and unrelenting poverty have set them up for a life 'on road'.

Some of the academic research into 'gangs' captures the way young people like this are in the 'here and now'. There is nothing to my knowledge which explains the origins of the beliefs, attitudes and behaviour of these young people in such depth or with such an unflinching commitment to the realities of their lives.

The teacher, the police officer, the judge and the surgeon are all genuinely concerned about these young people and, to an extent, they 'get it'. But ultimately, they are each left grasping for clichés, derived from their own experience of life and their own values.

However, what the young people present in Silent Voices does not lend itself to cliché. Rather, they offer us a grueling commentary on what life is like in the forgotten places the rest of us walk past every day, but though we walk down the same streets we walk though different worlds.

For anybody who wants to understand 'gangs', 'street worlds' or 'life on road' Silent Voices is essential reading. Anybody who wants to have an impact upon the psychological, social, cultural and economic factors that form the backdrop to the murder of Anton must read this book.

Introduction

Setting the scene

This story is based around a young man, Anton, whose affiliation and friendships with those caught up in gangs ultimately led to his murder. The story is told through the eyes of all of the people involved in this fatal incident, not just the members of the gang, but the teacher, surgeon, judge, and police officer, as well as the sister and girlfriends who were connected through this tragedy. The characters are an amalgam of real people that I have met during my 16 years of experience, working with hundreds of individuals and families whose lives have been affected by gang violence.

So although the characters are not real the stories are real. They portray the experiences and feelings that have been expressed to me, the raw emotions, the fears and ambitions that real people, affected by gang violence, have shared with me over the past decade and a half.

Although I have changed some of the background to the murder, the incident is true. This story is based on a young man called Sunday Essiet. Sunday was murdered in February 2008, hunted down by his killers in a park and stabbed multiple times, despite pleading with them. Sunday had a difficult life. He suffered loss at an early age. He was no angel. None of his closest friends would deny that. But despite the fact that the odds were stacked against him, he strived to move on. He was bright and had a sense of humour, but, most endearingly, he stood up for what he believed in and evoked and gave loyalty in equal measure.

Sunday was a young man with aspirations. He had a future ahead of him; not a mapped out future, but one that would have allowed him to experience life and touch the lives of others.

Most importantly, Sunday's death has made a profound difference too many of his friends, teachers, sister and the myriad of people who came to know him. It was a wake-up call to those closest to him; his "fam" or "bros". For many, his murder resulted in them making the first steps to walk away from gang violence. Some even went as far as mediating a truce with previous enemies. It was a brave decision, but with the support of Sunday's sister and his teacher, they achieved it in his name.

Sadly, Sunday will never know the difference that he has made. No one can hold him or congratulate him. But for those who got to know him, they will always remember him for enriching them through his life and by his death.

In essence, the location, time and date of the murder are incidental. They are merely the backdrop; the scene of an incident that could have happened in a park, a street, or a cold stairwell. Most importantly, all of the stories are true.

These stories provide a microscopic insight into the real issues and backgrounds that brought each of the characters to this one point. This is not the story of a reformed 'gangsta' turned good, or of the criminal lifestyle of those involved in the front line. Like Ed Burns' and David Simon's book 'The Corner', which sheds light on a year in the life of those that survive around a small block in West Baltimore, 'Silent Voices' tells the human stories of those caught up in the front line of Peckham; the pressures of life and the emotional baggage they carry with them. It tells of what brought them to the point of Anton's death and their perspective of then, now and in the future.

Silent Voices is a small social study of why people become involved in gang violence and the impact it has on our communities, told through the - often silent - voices of those involved, based in Peckham, in the heart of our capital.

Preface

Listen.

When you read the stories told by the characters in these pages, listen. Take a moment to hear them.

If you listen hard enough, as you read their journeys, hear their thoughts, and share their aspirations, you will recognise them: a friend, neighbour, brother, sister, or someone you work with. These are the voices of ordinary people, telling their extraordinary stories.

Whilst each of the characters was directly connected through this tragic event, the reality is that every character already had a connection. It was those connections that brought them to this single, life changing incident, as opposed to the incident itself.

These stories are the bare realities of those people whose lives are drawn together by gang violence on our streets.

Although the case of the trail following the murder of Anton has been concluded, the emotional pain that the family and friends have experienced has never been resolved. Their pain is so deep that they feel it in the marrow of their bones, a crippling, debilitating ache that turned them into invalids in the months after his life was so brutally taken from him. Time is an anaesthetic; it dulls the pain, but never heals it. Even years later, is comes back in waves of tsunami proportions, usually on anniversaries, or when they meet Anton's cousins or friends, all grown up and with families. Or, when the case rears its head in the media, when those found guilty are about to be released, having served 15 years of a life sentence (or for those under 18, just 8 years). Meanwhile the family and friends, the real victims, continue in a state of incarceration, of perpetual emotional lockdown.

In a perverse way, there is also no resolution for those that were instrumental in his murder. It is not because of any embittered sense of injustice, or from the perspective that because they have been caught, tried and found guilty, they feel that they have been unjustly treated. There is no resolution, because intellectually and emotionally they are now struggling to understand why, on that Sunday night in February 2011, they ended up being involved in the murder of someone who they once called their friend, someone that they grew up with, shared a sofa with, ate with, lent money to, and made an emotional bond with - so close they called him their "blood", "bros" and "brethren".

For those charged with the responsibility of dealing with the aftermath of Anton's shooting, there has also been no resolution. The sense of remorse of the school teacher who encouraged him to aspire and the surgeon who tried to save his life on the blood stained operating table is profound. Despite a lifetime of training and commitment to protecting young people and saving lives, they will have to live with the fact that all of that training, all of those hours, all of the personal sacrifices still was not enough to save Anton.

Then there is the investigating officer from the Metropolitan Police and the judge. They have moved on to the next case, the next intricate web of deceit that requires their expertise and knowledge to resolve. They have packed the boxes of transcripts; the evidence has been bagged and forensicated; conclusions drawn and judgments given. The case is closed.

But for their own personal reasons there have been things left unsaid. There is a stain, a blemish, which niggles at their conscience, not every day and not all the time. In fact, there are times when they can meticulously dissect the case and reassert justice. But in the night, or at the quiet times of contemplation, a grain of doubt worms its way back to the surface. It is a doubt which affects their personal judgment, impinging on the most critical factor; their ability to be impartial. Ultimately this will affect them in personal ways which they cannot foresee and cannot avoid.

There is one other person who we have not mentioned, someone whose guilt went unnoticed, but whose remorse is relentless. It was not a feud or disrespect issue, it was not a debt outstanding, or a drug deal gone wrong that resulted in their detached involvement. Although some of those people who knew her described it as 'love', it was not.

She is Anton's girlfriend, a tough streetwise tomboy who has lived out her life as a member of a crew that she latched on to at the age of 12. 'Girlfriend' is probably too strong a word to describe their relationship. It was not from a lack of desire on Anton's part. His ingrained family values of respect and care shone through. She was the one who resisted, allowing the resistance to soften at times, but never enough for him to get close.

Her involvement in Anton's murder was the fact that she did not do anything. She had a streetwise sense of what was happening that night but chose silence as her response.

Silence was a choice, her choice, one that still brings her pain.

All of the characters are real, a mixture of the genuine experiences told by the hundreds of people living in the shadows of gang violence. Every drop of blood in them, every emotion that is described and every infinite detail is as real as if they were standing next to you, telling you their story. The events they describe in their lives, every one of them, even those that you cannot believe are true, are true.

This is the story of Anton, through the eyes of those who knew him, those involved in his murder and those involved in bringing about justice. It is the story of personal perspectives; perspectives which provide us with the opportunity to recognise and resolve the real reasons driving gang violence in our cities.

Chapter 1
A Mother's Story

Look at me. Please don't look at the floor, look at me. Can you see me now through your brown eyes? Your eyes remind me of Anton's eyes you know. You have nice eyes, all shiny and full of life.

I could tell just by looking into Anton's eyes everything that was going on inside him, when he was happy, or sad, or was hurting. He was a happy boy you know, a kind boy to me and his little brother.

Did you know my boy? You must have seen him here? He often played on the street with his friends. Do you remember him? Perhaps you might have played football or basketball with him or seen him on the bus, or in school?

Here, I want to show you something. Will you take a look at these with me please? Here, bring your chair a little closer so you can see. I'm sorry, but my voice is not as strong as it used to be, I think it is the crying. Come closer. You see this picture? You know, this is my little boy; he was just three weeks old. You see him? He was a very small baby you know. Perhaps you were a small baby like him.

He was my first and I had a very hard time with him. My husband was not with me at the time and it was hard for me, setting up the flat, decorating and working. It was a hard time. But I knew that God was giving me a gift of life, so I wanted my child to have the best.

He was a small baby. He was born three weeks early, you know. Look, do you see how small his tiny hands were and his little wrinkled toes? He was just 5 lbs and half an ounce. When I first held him he gripped my little finger so, so tight. But I was not allowed to hold him for long. They put him in an incubator because he was so small. I used to sit and stare at him through the plastic cover, praying to God for him and praying that he felt my love for him.

After two weeks they let me hold him properly. I held him real close and kissed his sweet-smelling forehead and he opened his big brown eyes and stared up at me. My whole world changed then, you know. My heart filled my whole chest, as if God had entered inside me and filled me with love for this little boy. Can you feel the love I have for him? I bet your mum loved you just the same when you were born. Did she ever tell you?

Let me show you this picture here. This is Anton just before his fourth birthday. I love this picture. God blessed me with another child, Emmanuel. You see here, Anton, holding his little baby brother. This birth was very different than the first. Emmanuel came fast, he could not wait to burst into the world and meet his big brother. Will you hold the picture for me please? Look into Anton's face, can you see it? Can you see the love that is pouring from him for his new brother? It was as if he wanted to hold and protect him forever.

Don't be embarrassed, I can tell that you feel it, it's a good feeling. It means that God still has a place in your heart.

I remember something he said.
He said, "I think this is the best birthday present that God could have given me." I remember crying with joy and

hugging my two boys, thanking God for the love that he had brought to my house.

Do you have a little brother or sister? Perhaps you helped bathe them, or cream their skin so smooth and soft like Anton helped me to do with Emmanuel. He would help with changing and dressing him, losing patience with himself if he did not do it right, but never frustrated with his little brother.

Look you see this picture? This was my boy at the age of four and a half. This is his first day at Oliver Goldsmith Primary School. He was very proud of this day you know, his new blazer and shiny shoes. He polished them himself for half an hour. I thought he would rub the leather off with all that polishing. He tried to stand so tall that day, like a grown man and as I walked with him to school, he held his head so, so high. You know what he said to me that day? I will never forget it you know. No, don't look away, look at me. You know he said, "Muni, from today I will make you proud." As if I was not proud already!

You know he worked so hard at school. He studied and did his homework, but he did more. I did not even know what he did. Until one day at the parents evening, when he was 6, the teacher she say to me:

"Mrs Bakara, your boy is very special to us. He is an exceptional character, which we rarely see."

I said, "I know," but I did not really understand. I think she saw that in my eyes.

She said, "What I mean is, it's not about him being a bright boy, although he is. He just wants to please everyone, to help everyone. He helps the teachers prepare for the lessons, he helps the other students with their work, he even helps to talk to some of his class mates when they are sad. He is such a caring boy and everyone loves him for it."

Every time I look at this picture I remember every word that she said as if I am sitting right in front of her, soaking up what she is saying to me.

He had lots of friends you know. Here, look at this picture of him on a Sunday school trip and here, you see him with his football team? He was nine years old then. Do you play football? He loved football at school. I think you may have played with him at the cage or at the park. Sometimes he would come home with some of his friends after the match and they would fill the flat with their laughter. It was like a bright light of life filling our whole world. I thanked God for bringing us so much happiness.

It was a hard time for me. My husband had gone back to Nigeria. His father was ill. The money we sent over every month did not pay for the hospital bills so he had to go and look after him. But it had been four years now. He phoned every now and again and he always called on Anton's birthday. But money was hard.

When Emmanuel was two I got an extra cleaning job that paid cash. It helped a little, but I wanted to get a better job so I could give my boys more. So in the evening I studied to be a nurse. God helped me to get a small part time job in a care home. It was hard. I could not have done it you know, if Anton had not helped so much. See this picture? This is Anton taking Emmanuel to school on his first day.

When Anton went to the secondary school he felt he was becoming a real man, he was stepping into a new big world. He wanted to be the man of the house. Here, you see this picture? This is a very proud day for me. This is Anton's confirmation. We dressed up real fine you know, we bought special clothes from Rye Lane and a suit for Anton. Oh, so many people came, it was a joyous day. I had saved for a whole year to pay the church and for the food and clothes. But I was a qualified nurse now, working night shifts whenever I could for the extra money and keeping my little cleaning job going. On Saturdays, I would help clean the church and prepare for the service. It was my way of paying God a little bit back for all the happiness that he had brought me.

Anton still did well at his studies you know. Despite having to take his brother to school and being at home for him, he did well and had lots of friends. He never complained. He did not bring his friends round as much, but I knew he had lots of friends. He was always on his phone, or his computer, talking to them or sending messages. Sometimes they would ring in the evening and he would go out to meet them. He was a caring boy that way.

He never brought trouble to my door, always joy. There was one time, just one time you know. One day, I was in bed. I had just finished a shift and gone down for a lie-down. It was 5 or 6 o'clock in the afternoon. The bell rang but I was tired so left it. Then there was a bang, bang on the door, like Satan was trying to get in. I shouted, "Who is it banging on my door?" I did not really hear what they say, but I thought I recognised one of the voices as a boy from the church, one of Anton's friends.

When I opened the door there were four of them. They all had hoods on and caps, very disrespectful. I told them so and told them to go away, that Anton was not here. They said they would come back but I told them I said, "You do not come back to my door, I will call the police."

Then I saw the face of one of them, it was Jemaile, a good boy, whose mother I know from the church. "Jemaile," I said, "Jemaile, what are you doing banging on my door like this? What would your mother say? I shall call your mother and see what she says?"

The boys left. They did not come back.

This was the only day that I ever saw a change in Anton. When he came home his eyes were full of worry and fear. I told him about the boys but he said, "Muni, don't worry, it is sorted, don't worry." I believed him you know, Anton never lied to me.

He did not go out for a while after that. It was summer and he did not have school. His friends would ring him, but he did not go out. He was on his computer a lot and was reading. After a while, things just went back to normal. I did not want to ask Anton what happened, I did not want to upset him, you know.

I have another picture for you. You see this picture? This is the day Anton got his 'A' level results. You see how tall and proud he is. He was 6ft 1inch tall you know, such a handsome young man. He got 2 A's and a B, working so hard. He was accepted at Kingston University, not so far away so that he could still live at home with me. Emmanuel was 14 now and loved his brother. They would go out together, meet with friends. Emmanuel always had more to say than Anton. He would talk away with his friends and do music with them. Some of the words sounded like a different language. But my boys never argued.

I have two more pictures that I have to show you. You have been very kind to listen, to listen to me. I have nearly finished.

This is Anton in the hospital just after he was shot. He had all these tubes on him. It was February, did I say? I was working in the hospital on the ward when they came to get me. I thought they must have got the wrong Nurse Bakara you know. That was until I saw my boy.

He was in the emergency department. They were just sedating him. There was blood everywhere, on the floor and on the sheets. I have never seen so much blood, even on the wards. He was so still and quiet. All around him there was noise. The doctors and the nurses were busy all around him, but he was so quiet. I just sat there praying he would wake up but the pain of his silence just screamed out at me. It was an unbearable pain as if the devil were ripping at my heart. I held his hand and I think he   knew it was me, but I'm not sure.

I don't really remember the next few days. I stayed at the hospital and cried. I cried and prayed. I prayed to God to give my boy back to me healthy and strong. I prayed for him to protect him and heal him.

The surgeons worked so hard. They operated on him 4 times. He had been shot two times, in his shoulder and his stomach. The surgeons said that it had ruptured his liver. His potassium was very low and they were working hard trying to save him. The third operation they told me they had to remove his right leg, then his left leg, because of the potassium level which would affect his heart, such a strong heart, so full of love. I did not really understand, but I just wanted my boy alive.

It was two weeks that I sat at his bedside weeping and praying. After two weeks God took him. He took the life out of his eyes. I never got to say goodbye.

Silent Voices

Emmanuel misses his brother so much. He tries to be strong for me, but when I look at him, I can see that some of the life has gone out of his eyes as well. He does not do his music anymore and he does not talk with his old friends. He will go to university this September, to the same university that Anton was to go to. He is going for his brother.

Here this is my last picture. You see it? This is Anton's resting place. I bought a very fine stone. I had to save hard, but it had to be a special stone. Can you read the words? Will you read them out to me please?

"Yes, it says, 'Anton, a loving son and devoted brother. We love you with all our hearts but God loved you more and needed you by his side.'"

I don't cry as much now. I did not stop crying for a long time, but not so much now. But I have this huge weight right here where my heart is. It weighs so much that at times, many times, I cannot get up. I cannot breathe with the pain of it. On Anton's birthday or the anniversary of his death, the weight tries to break me. Can you feel my pain? Can you see it in me?

My church has helped and so has Emmanuel; they are a blessing to me. They tell me the pain will go but I don't know if I really want it to. I am frightened I will forget Anton if the pain goes. But I have these pictures, the ones I have shown you and telling my story helps me.

Anyway, I think our time is up. Thank you for listening to me, you are very kind. Perhaps we can talk again if you will let me. I don't feel angry or bitter you know; my faith helps. But just one question before I go please. Just one for you please.
"Why did you kill my boy?"

Chapter 2
Timi's Story

"I see no evidence in front of me that justifies this man being in the dock. Please release this defendant."

They had tried to break me. They accused me of things I never did, on the flimsiest of evidence, trying to prove my involvement, based on guesswork and fabrication. Ask anyone. Ask everyone that knows me. It's all made up, the worse kind of policing conspiracy, all based on prejudice.

Darell was my friend. So was Anton. I knew them both, ran with them when I needed, but they all knew that I had my studies, that I had a different plan in life. They respected that.

We moved twice in Peckham, my family and me, when I was young. I don't remember the first move, but I do remember the second. We were living on the Yellow Brick and I remember the paramedics and Police being in the house. I must have been five or six and my mum was screaming. Her face was a mess and her hands were covered in blood. This man had come to the door; I could smell the hate on his breath, mixed with the alcohol. One minute he had a bottle in his hand and the next there was glass everywhere.

Mum got taken to hospital and me and my brother went to stay with an aunt. I didn't even know we had an aunt. Later, when mum came back we were sent to a hotel, a kinda bed and breakfast place. I liked it. There were lots of new people but it was real noisy.

Silent Voices

Mum told me the man with the bottle was my dad. She didn't tell me that for a while, but I kept having nightmares about this man coming into our room and attacking us. She told me that he would never come back, or hurt us. I knew she was right. I vowed to myself that if he ever did, if I ever smelt him again, near my family, I'd kill him.

After that we ended up in a new flat in Rye Hill. The flat wasn't as nice and the stairs smelt of piss, but there was a big park nearby so it was better. I think I must have been seven when we moved there because that was the year I joined the football team - Dulwich Hamlets - and met Anton, Michael, KJ, Samuel and Darell.

We all lived off the Lane. Michael, Darell and I went to the same primary school, but we would all meet on the Rye, play football, or go round one house or another. I liked Anton's house best 'cos his mum was really warm and let us chill.

We just grew real close. If we had money we would share it, if we wanted to go somewhere we all went, if one of us had beef we all had beef. That's just how it was. You people want to label us as a gang. We were never a gang. We were just a bunch of kids who grew together and hung together. We were blood, that's what we were. We were friends and best mates, just like you've got best mates.

But people wanted to hang a label around our neck to make it easier, wanted to call us a gang, so they could pin stuff on us, give us notoriety before our time. That was their silly games, particularly the fedz, who seemed to want to call our names for any little madness that went down. You know they're the ones that created gangs, the fedz and then try turn us into gangs; real madness. If they had the tiniest bit of intelligence, they would have developed a good relationship with us, rather than punish us for being black and from Peckham.

When we went to secondary school things started to change. KJ, Anton and I went to Kingsdale. Kingsdale is south, right on the border of Lambeth, Southwark and Croydon. It's neutral territory in the main, but if there is beef it's personal stuff and then others get involved. When Shaks got killed - I mean Shakilus Townsend - it hurt us all. That Samantha was a hard bitch.

Kingsdale was a good school and I was bright. There was a teacher there, Ms Webster who got to know me. I remember her real well. She was the first teacher who really saw my potential. She gave me things to read, not like homework, just stuff she knew I would be interested in. I liked philosophy and then politics. The politics gave me the ability to contextualise the issues around me, to start to see how government uses power against local people in my area.

I was hungry for more. I used to stay on after school some days and research how the social changes of this country and America were influenced by politics. What I learnt was that political decisions were often made despite the impact on local communities, not to improve local communities. Anton and I used to talk about how we would use our careers to influence change. I'd go into politics and he would go into business and we would come back and make a difference for Peckham.

On the street my friends were still my friends. If you think that just because I was academic that this would change, you are totally wrong. We played football or sometimes went down the cage to throw some hoops. The football kinda faded away, except for Anton and KJ. They were really good at football. KJ had trials for Charlton and we were really proud of him. Most times we would meet up at Burger King at the top of Rye lane, on the front line and just chat and mix. We knew everyone. It really felt like our place, except for the fedz. We knew even then that the fedz hated us. We got stopped and searched all the time, even if we were just chilling. I remember this one time an officer called me a "fucking nigger" and shoved me against a wall. I could taste blood in my mouth. He was really angry when he didn't find anything on me, like he wanted to arrest me for any reason.

Then there was Michael. Now Michael had a real talent, a talent that talked to the masses and told things like they were for us in Peckham. He has music deep inside him and his bars were just awesome, real talent. He had an uncle who had a recording studio so we would all go down and hang out. Michael would do some spittin', always his own stuff. Then we would all do a bit of filming. Kinda "gangsta in da hood" stuff; nothing heavy. But the lyrics that came out of Michael's mouth. It cut me up, cut all of us up. He had a big following on YouTube that gave us notoriety, respect, because we were his people, his friends.

We never had any beef with anyone. We used to travel up west or east. There weren't any issues. KJ and I had friends from Kingsdale that lived in Sydenham and Norwood, even some in Brixton. So we used to travel. The whole postcode stuff is just a figment of people's imagination, another label by people who don't want to get to know us.

I don't really know what changed things. I don't really know if things actually did change. I was into the last year of my GCSEs. The fedz did a big raid in our area and some of the olders got picked up. None of the real players, they were too smart for that. But about ten or twelve of them, some of the foot soldiers and those that ran them. Taz, Medz, little Mike, even Tiny Sick, Sheldon and Fazer. Next thing Samuel's brother gets stabbed. Samuel texted me, really frightened that they would come after him.

Some man from the council turned up and then Samuel and his family got moved. He tells us he can't come back to the area, but after a while he does. But he had changed; he didn't want to do the music. He and KJ started hanging with some of the older boys. I knew them well. Geoffrey and Andre lived on my block and we used to talk sometimes about our families, sometimes football and girls. Andre went to the same church as me, my mum, Anton and his mum.

I was studying hard that year. I BB'd and talked through Facebook with everyone but we didn't meet regular. I saw more of Darell and Michael but sometimes I wouldn't see the others for a few weeks. KJ and Samuel were being given food (drugs) to deliver; sometimes local; but not always. I know they got trains to the coast, far west, all over. I think Anton got involved, I don't know why, perhaps just to get some stuff he needed. There was this girl that he was getting deep with, so knowing Anton he wanted to spoil her. He was stupid; he didn't have the stomach for supplying food.

I know KJ got caught once in Somerset. He was real angry with Anton over it, said it was his fault. But we knew it wasn't. Anton never had the bottle, and why take a 6ft frightened black boy into foreign territory if you didn't want to get caught? Stupid.

KJ got off. We all went to the trial, except Anton and Samuel. It was a joke. The local fedz had messed up again and the evidence wasn't strong enough so he was found not guilty.

It was the summer when I got a text from Anton. I had just finished my first year of A-Levels, in Sociology, Politics and Economics. When I spoke to him I could hear the fear come out of his mouth. Some boys had turned up at his house, youngers looking for some street rep. Anton wasn't in but he thought they were part of KJ and Samuel's crew. He said that Reefer, Tiny J and Jemaile were there. We calmed things down. I met with KJ and talked it through with him. We spent hours talking it through. We went to the studio and Michael and Darell were there. It was a long session, but KJ came round.

It cost us, though. See, KJ had lost a lot of food when he was arrested. He owed Andre over £200 for those wraps. It wasn't about the money but it was a big reputation thing and KJ knew Andre would have to come after him for it. Anton found half the money. I told him to and he knew he had to. The rest of us did some work for Andre. Nothing heavy, and I know Andre respected us for it.

I got on really well with Andre. I know he was an older but he was more like an uncle to me. He was 24. He had spent 3 years in prison - possession and firearms. His mum was a crack user, he never knew his dad, but he and his older brother were part of the original Peckham Boys. His brother wasn't in Peckham any more. He spent most of his time moving ever since he was shot in a night club on Old Kent Road. He had so much beef that he couldn't remember who his friends were anymore.

Andre was bright and he had a plan. His little girl was four by then. He was with her every day and he wanted a proper father-daughter relationship, wanted her to grow up respecting him, not seeing him as a street hood. He still loved the mother of his son as well. He never said it, but he kept talking about making her proud. He wanted to be a youth worker, but every time he went to apply he was told he had a criminal record and that he would have to wait. So he carried on earning by doing what he knew, but making sure he kept enough distance so that the fedz never had anything on him.

Andre and I would talk for ages. He was a real mentor for me. He told me all the time that I had to get to university; that I had a real brain and that I shouldn't waste it. He said that I had to prove it to everyone that people from the front line could make it, could achieve what they wanted to, that I would inspire others. He gave me a real sense of purpose and I knew that if I worked hard and used my intellect that no one would stop me.

Andre made sure that others knew I had a plan as well. That gave my studies a street legitimacy and gave me respect for what I was trying to do. There was no animosity between me and my friends. We met but, when I said I had to go, they understood.

KJ got shot. He was in a back of a car. It was a pool car, one of those cars you pick up from a street bay. He was in the back with Samuel when two guys on mopeds came up and shot through the window. Samuel said that it was a case of mistaken identity; that they were really after him. Samuel had got into some really heavy stuff. It was like he was trying to prove himself to his brother. Samuel had protection from some of the olders but he wanted more, so he and his brother, Tunde, had robbed an older of £15,000 drug money. Tunde had disappeared, probably gone back to Banjul. He probably thought his brother was better protected if he wasn't around.

KJ had been shot in the leg and stomach. Me, Michael and Darell all went to the hospital to see him. There was a police guard who stopped us seeing him, which really upset Michael and Darell. KJ's sister was there, she was crying so much that her mascara had run down into her mouth making long streaks like cracks in her lips. His mum couldn't come because she was ill, with MS. Some days she couldn't even get around the house. It was dusty and the furniture was all old fashioned like it came from a car boot sale.

There was a strange feeling in that house. Like everyone was waiting for something to happen, you could almost taste the anticipation. The sense of pain and death was almost stifling, and lingered over the place like a bad smell. Eventually we stopped going round there. That's why KJ tried to stay on road as long as possible: to get away from the stench of death.

After a while a consultant came out and talked to his sister and us, but I really don't remember everything that he said. I do know that one of the bullets had shattered his knee. I didn't realise it at the time, but the gun shot ended KJ's football career.

No one talked. The local fedz had a bad enough reputation but when the Trident Officers came in, that was another matter altogether. We knew Trident was against black people, that they would try to pin the crime on anyone one of us. So there was lock down. No one spoke and no one went out.

It was November, so the nights were cold anyway. It was my last year of A-Levels, so I just got my head down and studied hard. I applied for universities and got conditional acceptances at Kent and Essex. We BB'd each other and talked through Facebook. Michael posted a song about KJ. Me, Anton and Darell and some of the youngers were in it. It was really good. It got thousands of hits, as well as some stupidness from people who said we were challenging other gangs. Sometimes I think people misrepresent us solely for their own ends.

Next thing I know, Michael's been arrested for joint enterprise by Trident officers. Michael was KJ's friend. He wasn't even there. There was a lot of anger on the streets over that and it got people really on edge. You could feel the tension on the front line every time you went down there. The police had caused it but it was aimed at authority; all those people who didn't listen to us and treated us like we were a bad taste in their mouths, wanting to just spit us out, or wash us away. Anyway, Michael got bail and then the charges were dropped. Things calmed down, some of the elders and respected youth workers talked it through with us. Andre helped. He was working for St Giles, a charity in Camberwell that helped people coming out of prison. He was volunteering and studying at the same time and he and I talked about what was happening and how we could change things through politics and influence, not violence. Andre was a big voice for all of us and we listened to him real good.

There was a party at Christmas. I don't rightly remember whose house it was at, but I know it was on the Cossall Estate. I'd stopped going to local parties because of the madness. But everyone was going, Michael, Darell, Andre, all of the old crew. KJ didn't go - his head was all messed up after the shooting. Anton was there with this girl, one of the front line chicks that he kept chasing. It was all good, relaxed and like it was, back in the day. Then Samuel turned up. It must have been around 1am and things were in full swing. He turned up with some name from Camberwell way, someone who was acting as his muscle after his brother left. The whole atmosphere changed. Samuel acted the big man, demanding respect from some of the youngers. He started on Anton and there was a lot of beef between them. It started to turn nasty and we had to pull Anton out and get him to leave. Michael took him out, although Anton's girlfriend stayed. Samuel kept on shooting his mouth, like he'd given Anton a beating.

Eventually we left. It felt like the end of an era, like we would never be a group of friends again. I remember feeling like someone close to me had died but because it wasn't someone or something I could define, I wasn't allowed to grieve. I don't know how to explain it but I had lost something close to me.

It was 9.18pm exactly. I will never forget that time. I got a BB from KJ to say Anton had been shot. My phone got so hot after that, I couldn't keep up. I went down to the scene. The police had only just got there. Darrell was being taken off in an ambulance, he had blood over all over his shirt and he was being escorted by two police officers. He was so pale, wasn't kicking off or anything, just looked like the life had been pulled out from him.

I saw Michael. He was on the edge of it all, the scene and crowds, kind of like a ghost floating around all of the noise and heat that seemed to rise from the people. When I got to him he was shaking. I told him we should head for the hospital and check out Anton. He came with me but didn't say a word.

We sat in silence in the waiting room. It was full of drunks and crying kids. Anton's mum arrived with his little brother, Emmanuel. I don't know if she even saw us, she was wailing so loud. Emmanuel saw us, gave us just a small nod of recognition and then he and his mum were taken through into the bays, through the double doors that swung shut like they were being consumed forever.

We waited hours. We were tired and hungry but we just waited. There was a Fed that came and asked us some questions, but we didn't say anything. It's a free country, right, and we had every reason to be there.

It must have been around 2 or 3am when Emmanuel came out. He said that it was not good. Anton was in a critical condition. They had operated on him but he would undergo more surgery in the morning. He told us to go home; there was nothing we could do.

He asked us how come we knew what had happened, how come we had gotten there so quickly? I got angry with him. I know I shouldn't, but he knew there would be BB chat. Michael just stared at him and walked away. He had real anger in his eyes.

I don't rightly remember the next few days. I went back to the hospital a few times. There was loads of Facebook and BB madness, so I just ignored it and stopped looking. One day, when I went back to the hospital, they told me he was in surgery again and then I learned they took off his leg. I didn't understand what was happening.

Me, Michael and KJ put flowers on the estate where he got shot. There were loads of reporters but we just ignored them. I went to see Andre but he wasn't around, must have been working or something. The front line was deserted. One of the youth workers was out. I'd known him from back in the days and we always talked. He asked what was happening and we talked about Anton. He said the police were all over the area, as if I didn't know. But he also said that Anton's girl was real angry saying she knew who was involved. She'd been warned not to snitch but there was a lot of talk. I just ignored it, told him that I wasn't listening to all the noise, just praying for Anton. He told me to keep my head down; usual dumb advice, but I knew he meant no harm by it.

We tried to find out where Darell was but no one knew. He wasn't answering his BB and no one wanted to go round to the house. Someone said he'd been arrested, but no one was really sure.

It must have been like two weeks later when I heard Anton had died. The surgeons had cut him into bits, but they still couldn't save him.

There was a big public meeting with Trident and the council and lots of suited people who we'd never seen before. Harriet Harman turned up, minus her Met vest which made us laugh. She is the local MP and to be honest, we had respect for her. She helped a lot of our family friends from Nigeria who had immigration issues.

The meeting seemed as if the whole of the world's focus has suddenly found us like a lost tribe and wanted to make up for the years that they had consciously ignored us. I was reading a book on power and politics in Jamaica at the time, and was shocked by just how similar the reaction from the British establishment to Anton's death was.

Me and Michael went to the meeting. Anton's brother was there along with Trident, the top policeman for Southwark, some local politician and the MP. Not one black face on a table of power, looking at a sea of black faces. It spoke volumes. Anton's brother looked numb, like he couldn't take in what had happened. It must have been really hard facing all those people when his brother had just died.

There was press there as well, but no one spoke. No one said a word, not to the papers and not to the fedz. We didn't like the local police much, but we hated Trident even more now. Nothing had happened after KJ's shooting, no arrests, nothing. And now another one of our fam had been shot; only this time he was dead.

Anton's funeral was on a Friday. There was a big procession through Peckham after the church service. I couldn't believe there were some many people. We brought the whole of Rye Lane to a standstill. There must have been nearly 500 people. We crammed into the cemetery in Nunhead, under grey colourless skies which dulled the sombre faces, making the scene seem like some black and white film. There was a wake at the house after but we didn't go. Michael, KJ and I went to the studio. Michael started to record this intense track about death and life, like it was Anton speaking to us. I've never heard Michael spit a track like that before and I doubt I'll ever hear one again. It was an emotionally defining moment for the three of us.

Darell was still off scene. We got some of the youngers to go to the house but it was empty and no one was there. Seems the council had moved the whole family. His phone was dead and his Facebook page was down. There was a rumour that he was on remand and that the family had been threatened by some olders. Then there was other word on the street that he had snitched. I knew that was a lie, Darell would never snitch on his brethren.

Samuel was another matter. He wasn't on the front line but he was in deep. Facebook was hot with threats and challenges against him and by him. He seemed to love the notoriety. There was YouTube videos of him with girls holding shooters, covered in bling. With the streets so quiet no one would challenge him but some of the olders were getting really mad. But in Samuel's head, he was the man.

It was March now and my school life was coming to an end. I was doing some part-time work for a small charity linked to youth politics. It was inspiring. People listened to what I had to say and showed me respect for my intellect. By April I was studying hard, planning my revision, reviewing all of my course work. It was 9 - 5 every day, but I knew it was what I wanted more than anything else, a chance to really achieve, to go to university and prove that I could make it. It felt like the eyes of Peckham were on me, willing me to make it happen.

It was the 2nd May. I don't quite remember the exact time but it was around 6am. The front door caved in and the next thing I know I was pinned to the floor and in handcuffs. My eyes hadn't even focused and my mouth was dry, so I could hardly speak. But they pinned me to the floor and held me there for what seemed like hours. My mum was screaming. My brother was going mad, threatening the officers, shouting about police brutality. All the noise and the confusion smashed through my head and I didn't know what was going on.

Eventually, they pulled me up and told me to get dressed. They were searching my room, turning over every corner, going through all of my clothes. They had plastic gloves on like you see in hospital, like they were going to get contaminated or something.

They took me to a police station. I didn't know where it was to start with. It wasn't Peckham or Walworth. Later I learnt it was Belgravia. They put me in a cell. It stank of urine, sweat and alcohol. It brought back some memories and feelings of brutality and hate that I hadn't felt for a long while. It must have been a couple of hours when they came back and took me to an interview room. There were two of them and I remember how surprised I was that they seemed so young, couldn't have been much older than me, probably about Andre's age. They told me their names, but I don't rightly remember them; one was Robinson I think. I know they were from Trident and they said they were investigating Anton's murder.

Anyway they read me my rights and asked me loads of questions, like where I was, who I was associated with, what gang I was in. I knew all along that they had already judged me, so I didn't say anything. I kept silent; never said one word. Other boys from the front line had told us never to say a word in an interview with the fedz. So I just sat and listened to their questions and statements. They asked if I had a solicitor. I didn't say, but asked to make a phone call.

Eventually they took me back to the cell. No one came to get me and it was hours later that an officer eventually took me to a phone. I called my mum, but all I got was her voicemail. I left a message telling her where I was. I told the officer that I couldn't reach my mum and asked if I could make another call. He got really pissed when I asked this but eventually agreed.

I called my brother. This time I got through. I told him where I was and gave him the name of a solicitor. It was a good solicitor, one that several of the boys from the front line used. Andre and KJ had used him. He was from Brixton, but solicitors don't have endz, they just go where the money is. Anyway, after a few minutes this PC got really angry and told me to get off the phone. I just ignored him.

I finished my call and the PC took me back to my cell. He was really angry like I had ruined his life or something. He was just ignorant and I couldn't be bothered to say anything. After all I was the one has been jumped for no reason. I was the one locked in a cell with no explanation. So if anyone had a right to be pissed it was me. But I had to just play it cool, let them come up with what they wanted to say, otherwise try and stay cool. That was what all the boys had said.

It must have been about half an hour later when two coppers burst into my cell. It was the same PC and another one. The second one pulled me off the bed - some plastic mattress thing that every drunk in London must have sweated, pissed and thrown up on. The second PC wrenched my arm back, the pain was awful, but then he pressed his knee into my face and jaw. It felt like my eye was popping out. I tried to struggle but every time I moved my jaw felt like it was going to break.

There was this warm sensation on my legs. It was really odd and still makes me shudder when I think about it. It was strangely comforting at first like someone was pouring warm water over me to take away the pain from my face and arm. Then my head exploded as I realised what it was. The first fed was pissing over me. He was actually pissing all over my legs and trousers. I screamed but because my jaw and teeth were pressed into the floor the sound I made was like a rasping, muted breath.

I could hear one of the cops laughing, then, as I struggled to get up the other one said, "That will teach you to take the piss out of us, you black cunt."

I remember pulling myself on to the bed, my arm still screaming with pain and my head just spinning like I was inside some x-box game. The second cop was just staring at me. "Have you pissed yourself nigger?" he said, "You pissed yourself with fear? Won't be the first time will it? And where you're going, it won't be the last."

They left.

I don't really know what happened much then. I know my brief came and he went raging at the Trident cops. I don't think they were happy either. When I did get back into the interview suite the conversation was brief and they bailed me with a return date at the end of the month. My mum was outside in a taxi waiting to take me home, but the taxi driver refused to take me. I don't ever remember feeling so despondent in all my life. It was like I had been turned into something worthless, my whole life debased. We had to get three buses, with people staring at me and moving away when we sat near.

I threw all my clothes away. Didn't wash them or anything, just threw them out. I stood in the shower for what felt like hours, trying to get the stench of urine out of me. It was as if I could physically taste it, like it was rotting my tongue and throat. Every time I closed my eyes I saw that man standing over me, pissing on me and then I recognised who it was. It was my dad, standing there just like he stood there in front of me all those years ago.

They had taken the hard drive of my mobiles and computer and my laptop. The computer was old and was just a family thing. It didn't have nothing on, just photos and letters and stuff; it but they took it. My laptop had all of the course work, my A-Level stuff and two years' worth of notes; everything I needed for my revision.

I rang the Trident Fed. He didn't seem to care much, even though I told him how important it was. He said he would check it, but when he didn't ring the next day I called again. He said that I had to give him a list of everything I needed from the laptop and he would get it downloaded. I told him how hard it was to remember everything, but he said it was the best he could do.

So I did the list and sent it to him. It took them almost two weeks to even bother to get back what I needed and even then it wasn't everything. In the meantime I'd had to go to my school and get copies of course work and borrow stuff from my friends. I was too embarrassed to tell them why I needed it, just said my laptop had a virus.

I talked to my lawyer a lot. He was okay and at least he was on my side. He said that the police evidence was weak, that it related to a series of phone calls and texts made from my phone number. They had used GPS technology to pinpoint my phone to within 400 metres of the scene and at the approximate time that Anton got shot. I discussed with my solicitor just how flimsy the evidence was. It was all based on circumstantial evidence and there was nothing to say that I was at the scene and that it was even me that had the phone. I changed my phone regularly. I told him I wasn't there and he gave me his advice: to tell them where I was and who I was with.

We discussed it constantly over the next few weeks. But I had already made my mind up not to say anything to the fedz. I knew of lots of the boys from the frontline who had been arrested. They all said, "Say nothing." Even Andre said to say nothing. He said that every word I said would be turned and twisted, that they would try and catch me out or use it to incriminate someone else. He said that whatever I said would make me a snitch. There was no way that I was going to ruin six years of academic life and my future by being a snitch.

My mum was really anxious. She cried a lot and asked me to go to church with her and pray. I went. I didn't want to upset her. I had always been the strong one in the family, making sure I lived up to her aspirations, being the dependable one and making up for the pain my father had caused her. I didn't want her to worry, so I didn't tell her everything. I didn't tell her that I would say nothing, she wouldn't understand.

She really believed that the Police were honest people, people to trust. She still believed that the criminal justice system was an institution to be proud of, was the cornerstone of fairness and punished those who committed crime; part of God's instrument of justice on earth. She was so naive, but I knew it wasn't a view that I could change.

My solicitor was convinced that they would bail me. We went back to the police station on the 30th May. The same Trident officer interviewed me and there was another Trident officer, older and fatter, who said he was a DCI. They interviewed me for three hours. I said nothing, not a word. They kept asking me about where I was and my phones. They said my laptop had downloads of gangs, and I was a gang member. It was laughable. They were so dumb. Just because I kept some of the Facebook and YouTube clips didn't make me a gangster. They asked about my friends, other gang members and loads of stuff about Samuel and KJ. They were just so ignorant. I kept quiet. The only person who spoke was my solicitor, and he kept restating, "What actual evidence do you have against my client?"

Then they charged me.

They charged me with joint enterprise for the murder of Anton and attempted murder of Darell. I was in so much shock I couldn't speak; just couldn't get any words out. They charged me and remanded me into custody.

It was when they said that they remanded me into custody that finally woke me up. I said they couldn't, that they didn't have the evidence. I said I had my 'A' level exams in ten days' time - that they were trying to pin something on me just to ruin my life.

But the tables had turned. This time they had charged me. This time they didn't say a word. They just took me to a cell, and then in a police carrier to prison, Feltham.

I don't want to talk about the next few months. I just kept myself to myself. I kept my head down and kept away from any madness. My solicitor must have worked hard because they let me take my exams in prison. I sat in a room on my own and did all of the papers. In a strange way the fact that I was able to mentally focus on studying, doing the papers helped. I could use my intellect - the one thing that I knew set me above other people on the streets and in that prison.

There were other people in Feltham that I knew from the roads and from my group. I heard that KJ was there but in a different wing. I learnt that Samuel was also on remand but in a different prison. Sometime in August my solicitor asked me if I knew someone called Andre. He knocked me out when he told me that Andre had been arrested for possession of the gun that was used to shoot Anton. Appears the gun was in a bin chute cupboard near his flat, tucked away in a recess at the back. Some estate cleaner had found it when they were jet washing the area and had told the fedz. It shocked me to the core. Andre had kept low for so long and I knew that if he did have the weapon that he'd been told to hold it.

My solicitor had got me a barrister, a good one who seemed to really want my case. He said the evidence was purely circumstantial. He pressed me about where I was and when, who else may have seen me, the use of my phones. Most of all he pressed me about my friends. He made out that they were my biggest enemies. I talked with him long and hard, about what it was like growing up in an area, that these were my friends from back in the day, that just because I chose to meet with them didn't mean I was a gangster or a criminal, and it certainly didn't mean I would kill my friend. We talked for hours. It was a relief from the other madness of being in jail.

The trial was in November. I had been held on remand for nearly six months. It took place at the Old Bailey at the Criminal Law Courts, Court 13. When I was brought to court I was held in a small cell and then taken to the dock. It was the first time that I had seen KJ and Samuel. We all acknowledged each other. KJ kept his head down, but Samuel stood up tall, started waving to people in the public galleries. It was packed. Some of the olders and youngers were there and family. My mum was there. She was there. Michael's mum had come with her for support. There was some press and then some reserved seats. The whole court went quiet and when I looked up again I saw Anton's mum and his brother come in. I felt too ashamed to look her in the face.

The next thing Andre was brought in. The blood seemed to have drained out of his face and he looked like he had shed pounds. He didn't look at us, at me. He just kept his head buried into his chest, like he wanted to disappear.

When the judge entered, we all stood up. It was something we did every time he came in or got up, every day, for the six weeks of the trial. It was almost like an act of a play when the curtains come down or go up, announcing the next piece of theatrical drama.

There were so many procedures to go through on that first day that by the end of it, there hadn't been a single witness or piece of evidence presented. But eventually the prosecution started listing out all of the charges relating to the night of Anton's shooting. They talked about the evidence that they would produce; the witnesses and forensics. I don't remember all of it but the bit that really stuck with me was when they said that this group of known gang members "premeditatedly" went out to "gun down" Anton. It was so far from the truth that it was laughable, except we were the ones who seemed to have to prove our innocence rather than they had to prove our guilt.

The trial went on and on. All the lawyers questioned the witnesses which took forever. My name didn't get mentioned much but I was getting really frustrated when my barrister just sat back and didn't say a word. I began to get the feeling that he was actually setting me up. When I did talk to him at the end of each day, he told me that it was all about choosing the right moment. He said that the fact they had made little reference to me meant that their evidence was potentially unfounded and highly questionable.

It was about two weeks into the trial when the Trident officer gave evidence. After he had been cross-examined by all of the other barristers my lawyer stood up. He asked about the evidence and the phone evidence. The Trident fed seemed almost belligerent. He said that the GPS evidence pin pointed the phone number, my phone number to the scene. But my lawyer didn't give it up. He kept on pressing him on the accuracy, whether the phone number was really my phone number at the time.

The next expert was a specialist investigator in telecommunications. My lawyer pressed him again and again. The specialist eventually caved in and admitted that the GPS was only accurate up to 50m. It was like watching a crocodile get the kill as my lawyer tore into him and the prosecution saying that they had brought his client to this court on the flimsiest of evidence.

Then the judge started asking the prosecuting lawyer about what other evidence that they had on me. There was a long conversation between them and the judge looked really angry. When the judge stopped the conversation he turned to the jurors and said,

"I can see no evidential reason for this young man to have been brought to this court in front of this jury. Any evidence is not sufficiently grounded in fact to allow this person to remain on trial. Timitao Obeseymi, you are free to go."

I didn't really know what to do until a police officer led me out of the dock and out of the court. My mum was outside and she couldn't stop hugging me and crying. My brother was there too and my lawyer. I was in shock. I remember phoning lots of people and then we went home, people came round, it was constant. All I really wanted to do was sleep.

I went to the trial every day. I didn't tell my mum but I went every day with some of the olders. Samuel was found guilty of the murder of Anton and attempted murder of Darell and KJ for joint enterprise. Samuel got thirty years, KJ got fifteen, and Andre got nine years for possession of a firearm and perverting the course of justice. I felt really bad for all of them, they were my friends, but I felt worse for Andre. Everyone on the streets knew that he had been forced to hold the weapon. They were going to kidnap his baby and rape his girl and he knew they meant business.

The next few months were really hard. I kept busy at first, applying for universities and trying to get some work. Some guy from the council came round and got me some part time work with an organisation in the city. I moved out of Peckham, just to give me the space to get my head straight. I got university offers but my grades weren't as good as I expected. I only got one A and two B's, so the points weren't high enough for the course I wanted. So I arranged to do a 12 week course in philosophy and politics and then go to UCLAN. It was a place where lots of other people who were involved in politics seemed to be going. Most of all I wanted, more than anything, to focus on the plan I had set myself. I wanted to prove to every Trident officer that they couldn't break me, that I was better than them and their stupidness.

But after about three months it hit me. I started to think about what they had done to me, how the whole system had tried to break me and ruin my life. They wanted to use their prejudice as a stick to beat me down, just like they had tried to beat down every other young black person from my neighbourhood. I spent a long time talking it through with people, particularly the guys I worked with, who seemed to really empathise. This one guy gave me lots of time and gave me lots of books to read. Those books became like food and drink.

There was one book called 'Crime and the American Dream' that I read that really made me realise that if I want to change the political system, I had to be in the political system. It talks about how politicians in America developed social culture and social competition through aspirations; aspirations based on how you should live your life but embedded in them the aspiration to have the right material things. They intertwined. Having the right stuff was a sign of having the right moral and social attitude. If you don't have the right stuff, the most up to date stuff like the latest model of car, fridge, TV, right clothes and so on, you aren't socially and morally aspiring and you aren't living the American Dream. Those that aspired achieved and those that didn't got left behind.

It was a powerful influence for me because I could relate to this in what I saw happening in Peckham. Do you get me? People in Peckham, like my friends, are getting left behind, because politically and socially they aren't being recognised. The political system ignores them.

I start my 12 weeks course in September, and then I'm off to UCLAN in the New Year. I'm not bitter for what's happened to me. Life is full of learning and I have learnt enough already to know that I have the courage and intellect to change things, starting with the culture of prejudice and ignorance.

I never want to repeat going to jail. If anyone asks what it's like going to jail, tell them it's the most degrading experience in life. I've learnt that from bitter experience, and some of my friends are still in jail and their lives are over, just like Anton's. Andre's girlfriend has moved away and she doesn't visit him anymore. Samuel's younger brother is running lines and some of the madness has started again. I still see Michael, but it's not the same; too much history.

I visited KJ and we talked. He seemed resigned to what he was facing. What neither of us can reconcile is that despite all of the police work, everyone in the community knows that the person who actually pulled the trigger and shot Anton is still out on the streets, whilst KJ is serving time. Where is the justice in that?

Chapter 3
Our Endz

There has been an ongoing debate over three decades in how best to define the dynamics, the underlying issues that drive gang association, gang affiliation and gang violence. These dynamic factors are not independent, in the same way that the characters involved in Anton's murders are not independent. They are the DNA, the building blocks that bind together to form the genes that define us. But understanding each of the five dynamic factors provides the greatest opportunity for change; a chance to realign our moral, social, political and emotional compasses and to really address the grip of gang violence that exists across parts of our communities.

The first of the five dynamic factors is the environment.

The environment for this story is Peckham; an area like so many in London that has been shaped by the people that live and breathe within its borders.

Peckham, or any of the locations that are affected by gang violence, provides an ever-evolving backdrop, which reinforces the perception of personal inequality. Densely packed housing estates are bordered by tight, congested roads leading into run-down retail areas, where the volume of sales overrides the quality of what is being sold. Chic becomes shabby and if you have the money to go up West to buy quality, you might as well live in the suburbs for the amount of time it takes you on the tube or train, or bus:

inadequate public transport that fails to make up for a decent underground line.

As London evolves and changes, so does Peckham. Led by property developers who recognise that if they pitch the marketing just right, they can attract a more affluent clientele. As they take a hold in the surrounding areas of Nunhead, Bellenden and Peckham Rye, the new wealth and socially connected community becomes a further reminder to those growing up on the estates that their ability to bridge the gap from the life they live to the life they aspire to live, has never been more unattainable.

Let's take a closer look at Peckham.

Think of the area like a living organism - a human body. The housing estates are the heart, pumping out its residents daily along its network of arterial roads; flowing into the sinews of shops and schools; feeding onto buses and trains where commuters muscle for space; going out to earn a living that continues to feed the life blood of the area. As one part of the body tires - trudging back to gain much needed sleep - so the area spews out a new mass of people; rejuvenated, working through the night to make sure that every ounce of effort is maintained to keep itself alive.

History has changed this area, this one small environment which makes up the urban sprawl of London. Once an affluent suburb, it has been swallowed up, bound up into a throng of housing estates, congested roads and a multitude of people, hustling for space, for a sense of purpose and recognition that they are individual, amongst a mass of 11 million people all competing for that small grain of personal acknowledgement. And yet, within the all-consuming amorphous mass that makes up the capital, the human body of this microcosm manages to retain its sense of individualism.

This is Peckham. Its name will conjure different visions within you, just like any name. For those of you who have never been introduced to Peckham let me tell you a bit about her.

Let us start with the town centre, a bustling hive of a high street called Rye Lane, full of colour and life: a handful of chain stores set amongst busy local businesses, vying for similar business. The smell of halal butchers catches the back of your throat, closely followed by the toxic combination of chemicals from nail bars and hair products. Both disguise - but cannot block - the smell of rubbish and discarded food that emanates from the overflowing commercial waste bins.

The semi pedestrian area to the north of Rye Lane merges with the narrow, tightly congested streets of the south, where traders encroach onto the pavements in a desperate bid to entice customers, whilst customers desperately try to keep to the ever narrowing pavements. Here the Asian and Afghan shopkeepers ply their trade, trying to manage the fine balance between giving the customers what they want, whilst at the same time protecting their business from petty street criminals.

There is tension here: a bitter rivalry of mistrust between communities and businesses, grown out of a sense of commercial injustice. This injustice has its roots in the perception that the shop keepers have the money and the police protect them. It simmers, threatening every now and again to boil over and create a racial divide between the shopkeepers who have, and the black Afro Caribbean residents who want. The reality is that their distrust all boils down to money.

In the end the threats and intimidation die down because these two fractious communities are ultimately united by the much greater challenges of social and economic injustice. They are part of a community, intent on survival, getting through the daily hardships, eking out every penny, intrinsically intertwined through an acknowledged dependency on one another, in finding ways of getting by.

Two indoor markets are full of tiny shop units selling products that no one really wants but everyone seems to have, at knockdown prices. The busiest shops are Poundstretcher and Primark; the busiest businesses are the nail bars and hairdressers, whose numbers seem to expand on a daily basis. But the real growth businesses are the money lenders, the pay day loan specialists who promise a golden today, paid for tomorrow, to people who still believe in 'mañana'.

A cinema and Rye Lane Railway Station sit opposite each other, both offering escapism, even if it is just for a few hours, until the reality of life brings people back to the bosom of Peckham.

To the north of Rye Lane is Peckham High Street. The Job Centre and Burger King hold court over smaller businesses - chicken shops and fast food outlets, clothes shops that sell designer wear from forgotten designer labels.

This is the front line; a small run of about 400 yards where the street hold those from 'da streetz', where a collection of young men and women compete for status and respect amongst their group, but hold fear amongst their peers. Their individual faces tell a very different story - a personal pain from years of holding their personal emotions in check - hiding it from everyone but themselves. For the moment we will pass this group by; you will know more about some of them later, but for now let's leave them in the knowledge that they are safe in each other's company.

Business is thriving in Peckham, on the front line and on the Lane. Money is being made and 'work' is being done. But it is not the legal businesses that are thriving. Legal businesses are trying to squeeze out the pennies that mean survival rather than profit. It is the illegal businesses which thrive: trades on mobiles and laptops; experts who can unlock phones and bypass security; counterfeit goods and under the counter food products that are exclusive to the area; store cupboards at the back of shops and loft spaces converted to offer low rent for illegal workers; cheap labour who can afford no better.

Right in the heart of this is the drugs market, holding a vice-like grip around Peckham's throat, attempting to choke the life out of her. The drugs market set the tone, injecting a daily dose of poison into the area, and defining the volatility on the streets. This is the territory where relationships are quickly formed and violently broken; where feuds over monies owed and disrespect are violently settled for the price of a misplaced bag of skunk.

It is the drugs market that draws the line between friendships that turned to enmity, replacing shared laughter and close bonds with knives and guns. The constant pressure of selling to make money, to pay back your supplier plus their mark up; the paranoia of being caught or your stash being stolen; who to trust and who you might be in conflict with, all these thoughts continuously running through their minds every day, creating a level of anxiety which quickly turns to personal feuds and disrespect. The drugs markets have left victims scattered across Peckham, some still marked by decaying flower tributes, from families who have not forgotten them and seen by puzzled commuters who never remembered them.

This is where our story starts. This is where it ends.

Peckham has not grown old gracefully. She has been rejuvenated, given a face lift and some botox to iron out the wrinkles and lines. Peckham Square lies just beyond the High Street, bordered by Peckham Hill Street and Sumner Road. Built in the 1990s by a world famous architect, it received the 2000 Stirling Award for architectural innovation. Peckham Library strikes an impressive pose; its 5 storey L shaped design dominating the Square and dwarfing the leisure centre. The old tower blocks that used to look over the area have long gone, demolished as the century ticked over, and replaced by low level brick houses, flats and play parks.

The Damilola Taylor Centre is set in the heart of this regeneration. It is a poignant reminder of one of the darkest moments in Peckham's history. But it is a place of real hope; a safe place for those who use it; a place that has helped open doors for many other young people during its 11 years of life; one more than was experienced by its namesake. Damilola would not recognise the area if he saw it now.

The physical changes to Peckham have redefined her character. Smart rows of houses and low rise apartments are interspersed with internal courtyards and small green spaces - a physical regeneration, designed to change the identity of Peckham and attract some new suitors. Yet whilst the regeneration has acted as a catalyst for change, with better quality low rise homes and open play spaces, the retail areas, roads and transport have not caught up. As a result, the best intention of providing an environment where communities can prosper has turned into areas where communities are retained. The future is bleak when it takes half an hour to travel less than a mile and the most accessible retail shopping complex is on the Old Kent Road.

Sadly, the first decade of the new century did not bring any respite in violence for Peckham. The area alone experienced over a dozen teenage murders during those 10 years. Each one leaving a deep wound, exposing her emotional fragility, damaging her reputation, leaving her more vulnerable and her community grieving another loss; an unstoppable weakness which every newspaper and media crew took full advantage of.

Some of the older estates still exist, dotted around the town centre acting as guardians. Some like the Yellow Brick, Cossall, the remnants of the north Peckham Estate, or Friary, have a notoriety, a toughness of their own: "Don't mess with da Yellow Brick."

A one way system cuts down the east side of Peckham Rye, eventually leading its way to Peckham Rye Common, a huge triangular shaped open space where people can once again take a deep breath of relief from the intensity of the Lane.

Harris Academy @ Peckham is to the west of Rye Lane, a few yards along the High Street and just off the front line. Young people enter with high aspirations, looking for the nuggets of education and insights that will move them on and get them out. The Academy is their best chance; possibly their only chance. Those that come to teach want success and those that come to learn want to be successful.

But life is not that easy. For some the daily pressure is not an academic one. For some the pressure is just life; a sibling that needs to go to school; a mum who is ill; a dad who is not around; a flat where the sitting room is a bedroom and the bedroom is shared by you and your brother, or worse your sister. There is no space to study and there is no space for privacy; no space to think; your identity is lost. The street is the best escape, where the emotional pressures of life can be hidden, replaced by different emotions based on instinct and fuelled by personal status. Here you can forge a reputation, even if it is not a reputation you really deserve or ever desired.

Further west of the Academy, running south from Peckham Road is Lyndhurst Way; the start of a myriad of streets lined by Victorian Houses and interconnected parks. The roads weave in a one way system designed to confuse and bemuse drivers, whose desire for a short cut is quickly cut short by unannounced dead ends, and dumbfounding double backs.

Nestling in the heart of this knotted Victorian enclave is Bellenden Road and Bellenden village. Once a side road running parallel to Peckham Rye, it is now one of London's more fashionable areas, with a handful of chic shops, delicatessens and restaurants. It is a place where artists and high-flyers have replaced older families, renovating and rejuvenating their homes, telling their work colleagues about the excitement of living in gritty, edgy Peckham, whilst demanding the estate agents market their homes as 'exclusive Bellenden Village'.

The commonality amongst all the places that breed gang violence - whether it is in London, Manchester, Birmingham, Baltimore, LA or Chicago - is that deprived areas create an atmosphere of suppressed ambition, where the challenges that families face is reflected in the grubby streets and unpainted buildings; piled up rubbish in the street; discarded mattresses, fridges or washing machines by the bin chutes on the estates; electrical goods that were bought cheap and broken quickly by a family who just could not afford anything better.

There is an atmosphere in Peckham. You will feel it from the moment you arrive. You can actually touch it and you can see it in the faces of the people around you. It is an edginess that is not fear or intimidation; people do not have time for that. Nor is it vibrancy, although it has a distinct sense of being alive. It is expectation; an expectation that at any moment something will happen, something that will define today in the life of Peckham.

Everyone moves with a sense of purpose and if you look into their eyes you will see that they are alert, aware of what is around them, anticipating what might be ahead of them, and trying to avoid what is behind. Things need to be done; not big things, just the stuff that gets you through today, gets you home safe and into bed so that you can start again tomorrow, and again the next day; a daily survival that continues day by day by day.

And yet despite the cacophony of issues that scream from every shop and doorway, street corner and classroom, there is ultimately hope. There, right in the archway to Peckham Square is the Peace Wall, a lasting reminder of the dark days of the summer riots in 2011. The Peace Wall is smothered with messages of love for Peckham, of hope for the future, bold defiance against those that might try to sully her name, or dishonour her virtue. Despite everything, "I love Peckham", because despite everything she has been through, Peckham has the endearing capacity to forgive everyone.

Peckham has a history and a present. So what about the future?

You would be forgiven for feeling sorry for her, because we have painted a picture of an area stumbling to get to her feet. But Peckham does not want your sorrow, or your pity. Peckham has a bright new future, full of bright young people who have so much to offer. They are entrepreneurs with business skills, shining personalities, full of vision and ambition. They are politically and socially aware, with the ability to articulate what needs to change and how it can change for the good.

They are not frightened about the future. What they are frightened about is that others, outside of Peckham, will give up on them, not give them a chance, or worse still, offer some false hope which draws in their trust and then forgets them if it does not quite work out. The environment reinforces their perception as they see other areas regenerated. New jobs created in business and commerce in areas just over a mile away, but which could be on another planet.

They watch this expansion, in the hope that it will provide opportunities. They see new developments, new homes, new hope, a chance that somehow, with someone's help they can make it. What they experience, what surrounds them is their reality of tough streets and dependent families, where prospects are about working hard, just to get by.

What they want, what Peckham wants, is to give them a chance. Park your prejudices of the things you have heard and not experienced, and shine a spotlight on their ambitions, their hope and their ability. Give them a chance. Give them a small grain of an opportunity, so they can fly.

Silent Voices

After all, what have you got to lose?

Chapter 4
Selina's Story

I don't know why you are wantin' to talk to me. It's like I never really knew nothing of what KJ was doing, right. I like heard stuff but he was my brother and like, he had his stuff and I had my stuff.

KJ was always like the little man in the family. Dada used to call him "little man", like, trying to make him into someone important. But he was only 5 and it was like really funny, him trying to boss us. If he got too big in them grown up boots that Dada was making for him, I'd just pinch him really hard on the arm. I could like twist the skin so hard and then he would start crying. It was pathetic.

I am the second oldest. My sister, Patience, is 2 years older than me and KJ is 4 years younger.

I was, like, really happy where we lived. We lived in the house on the North Peckham estate, just off Sumner Road. I know we moved around a bit before, but I only really knew this house, right. We had a little garden; nothing much but it was like really cool 'cos none of my friends had anywhere like it. Most of my friends lived in the flats, but they are from all over. My friends are in Peckham and Brixton, some are north and east. It's not like we can't go anywhere; not like some of the boys. They need to take some air.

The church was a big, big part of our lives. Mama believed in the Lord like he was in the room with us every day. We went to an evangelical church on Choumert Road on a

Sunday and a Wednesday. Patience and I loved the church. We were in the choir and we would sing our hearts out. We prayed real hard to keep us all safe and for the Lord to help us make Mama proud of us. We had lots of friends from Sunday school and some days they would come back to our house and the rooms would be filled with laughter and chat and we would all sing 'til the neighbours complained.

When KJ was about 8, Dada stopped coming around. I don't rightly know why. He wasn't as interested in me and Patience much anyways. It's not like he lived with us or anything, but he always bigged KJ up. He would take him places. I don't rightly know where and I don't care, but KJ was dead keen.

Sometimes Dada would call and tell KJ he would come on Saturday and take him football, or to Maccie D's or down Nandos. Sometimes he would come late and KJ would have been waiting on the door step for like hours. Other times he wouldn't show at all and KJ would go all deep and quiet. I told him daddy didn't really love him and that he only turned up so he felt less guilty. It's true you know. But KJ would get all aggressive and try to beat me. I would just laugh and slap him down.

Once, KJ and I saw Dada with another woman and some kids. They were his kids of course. Anyway KJ saw him and smiled. I reckon Dada saw him too 'cos he like turned away. KJ got real upset then. I don't rightly know why 'cos everyone knew Dada had at least one other family. It wasn't like it was a secret.

Anyway just after that Mama started gettin' sick and Dada didn't turn up anymore. We would see him around every now and again over the years but it was like seein' a ghost.

I was just starting my GCSEs and Patience was in sixth form. We were at Harris Academy in Bermondsey. We both loved school. Patience got A's and B's in her GCSE's but I knew I was brighter than her so I set out to beat her. Back in the day I was, like, real competitive. I was really good at sport as well. Runnin' was my thing and I was as fast as the wind. The best of thing was beatin' KJ. He liked football but he wasn't that good. I would take his ball and run off 'cos he couldn't catch me. It was real funny.

Mama's sickness wasn't a sudden thing. It was like really slow and we didn't know for ages what it was. She would get pains in her eyes and numbness so she, like, couldn't get up. Then a day or so later she was ok. Or she would complain of being stiff and then it would wear off. She went to the doctors like a hundred times. It seemed to go on forever. Then she was sent to the hospital. Not the one where all the gang boys go to get patched, but the one near the river, Guys and St Tommies. Patience went with her and it was like all day.

I had to get KJ from school. I know that day really well 'cos KJ had got into a fight and he had detention. I was like really angry with him 'cos I had to wait like forever. I chastised him like Mama would and told him he brought shame on us when Mama was sick and could die. He started crying. It was real pathetic.

Anyway Mama had MS - Multiple Sclerosis. We didn't really know what it was. The doctors had told Mama but she didn't have a head for rememberin' all what they said. Patience looked it up on the computer. It's like to do with the muscles and stiffness, like, spasms and stuff. She said it was like the parts of your body that keep you healthy attack the parts of the body that make you function every day, or whatever. Looking back I didn't really get it then, but I understand now.

We would all help out and it wasn't too bad at first. Mama had lots of hospital appointments and treatment, but as time went on it like got harder. Patience went to university, but she carried on living at home 'cos of the cost. She went to London Metropolitan University and studied history. She wanted to become a teacher but she also wanted to get a degree first. She was studying hard so she didn't have time to help much. I was doing my A-Levels and it was hard with all of the course work and stuff.

Mum had to stop workin'. It was like ok to start with. We got extra benefits and stuff but it got hard. Some days we wouldn't have any food to eat just because we couldn't afford it. KJ got real mad when this happened, like we did it just to annoy him. He seemed to think that he had to make up what we couldn't do, like he was some kinda "big man" provider, rather than a little boy who was like, only just out of shorts. I put him straight and told him to have more respect for Mama.

Mama started having problems with the stairs, so after a while we set up her bedroom in the living room. Me and Patience were real pleased 'cos she moved into Mama's room and I moved into Patience's room. KJ had my old room and didn't have to share with Mama anymore but he still complained. Like, anyone would think that we hadn't done him a favour.

KJ could have done more around the home but he was lazy. The washing up got left and the cleaning. We had a big row once when he brought some of his wannabes round. I told him he better get out of my face or like, I would slap him down. KJ had rights but in the house he had to earn his rights and back then he was in the red.

KJ stopped bringin' his friends round. I was real pleased 'cos it meant they would stop stinkin' out the place with their laziness and spliffs. His room stank of spliffs. So he stayed out more and would come back like, late, late. Some days he wouldn't come back. I don't know where he went to do his madness, but he didn't bring it back to our door. He would have been like 16 or 17 then. I don't rightly remember but I know he didn't get up in the morning and missed loads of school. Patience and I told him how foolish he was but he stopped listening. I couldn't beat him anymore; he was like 6ft. The only thing that got him out of bed was his friends and his football. He was ok at football I suppose. He got into Charlton but then who are Charlton? It's not like Arsenal or Chelsea is it!

I was at a nursing college over West. I had decided to become a midwife. I knew from the days of helping Mama that I wanted to go into nursing, but I also wanted to bring new life into the world, like, makin' it better. Patience was 23 or 24; she had just done her teaching qualification and had a post in a primary school in Croydon - she was really happy. We would like chat all the time and helped mum with her bathin' and food. Patience was like my best friend. We would go out together if we had time, but the best times were just sittin' in together in one of our bedrooms, like, just chattin'. Patience got serious with this guy; he was a teacher at the school, very respectable, just what Mama wanted.

Mama was real proud of us. She filled the house with pictures of us, in our school uniforms, at our confirmations or graduations; pictures of Patience with her man. We wanted to make her so proud, to take away the suffering that she had. I love my Mama like I want to burst some days.

Mama's MS started getting really bad and seemed to last, like, forever. I couldn't even get her up some days to go church. The pastor was a good family friend; came from the same region in Sierra Leone as our family. He would come round and would talk to her. It helped at first but then we had to stop it, because the pastor said we had to pay the church for the extra visits as it was like an extension of God's house. With Patience only just startin' work and me at nursing college, we couldn't afford it. We still went to church and prayed to Jesus for Mama and on the days she was strong enough she would come with us.

KJ stopped comin' to church. Mama asked him to, like a hundred times. He never rowed with Mama but on the church stuff, he just disobeyed her wishes. I told him how much he was letting her down and like he was disrespectin' her. He said that Jesus didn't even care for us and if he did he wouldn't put Mama through so much suffering. I told him that the only person makin' Mama suffer was him and to shape up.

That year KJ got arrested. I don't rightly know all of the details. I didn't really ask. Some police officers just turned up one day with a warrant. I wasn't even at home at the time. Patience got back from teachin' and they were in the house searchin' his room. They found some skunk and a knife. They said the skunk was enough for possession with intent to supply. It didn't surprise me.

Mama was real upset. She was cryin' and beggin' with the police to leave her son alone. Like, she got herself so worked up that she became really ill and we had to call an ambulance for her. But I knew the police just had to do their jobs. It was KJ who was the problem, not them, and I told them right in front of him to like arrest him and lock him up, to teach him a lesson.

Later we found out that KJ had actually been arrested in a place called Taunton. It was a long way away and I don't rightly know how he got the money to go there. He was with this low life gangsta boy called Samuel. I didn't like Samuel. I knew him 'cos he hung around outside Burger King in Peckham and I saw him there with KJ. He acted the tough guy. Some of the girls from the area used to like hang with them but they weren't my type. Like the girls were so cheap and their make-up was like really bad.

Anyway, KJ got bailed and was put on a curfew. I don't know why they bothered because he didn't go out for like ages after that; he acted real weird. His phones would go off and he would use those short, one word replies. If anyone came to the door he got like, real stressed. He probably owed someone some money or something, but it was like his own problem right, for hanging with gangsta boys and pretending he was like some kinda tough man.

Anyway it soon stopped and he went back to his old ways.

Some of his friends came round and seemed to talk some sense into him for a short while but he was too dumb to take any real notice. After that he stopped bringin' anyone back to the house. He stayed out late, sometimes for days on end. I don't rightly know where. No, I didn't ask because I didn't care much, as long as he didn't like bring any more trouble to our door.

He kept changing his phones all the while and the only person he really seemed to hang with was Samuel. He must have like stayed over at Samuel's. He never said, but he never seemed to want for anything. He had good clothes and also ate well, 'cos he constantly talked about going out to work, or to get food.

Patience moved in with her boyfriend that autumn. They rented a place down in Sydenham, not big, but it was great for them. It was a lot easier for work and I would go down like every week and we'd meet up at weekends; when I wasn't studying or working that is. I was placed on a ward in a hospital in Paddington, as part of my training. It was the best. I really liked the staff and the work was good, although some of the patients could get like real annoying.

We got in some help for Mama. We went through social services and it like took forever. They lost the forms and then had to send someone around to assess her needs. It was real painful. But we got someone who would come in and help bathe Mama, change her clothes and like, help her with food and stuff. When I worked nights we got friends from the church to come in and check Mama was ok. It was like real hard, but the worse thing was I couldn't take Mama's pain away. I prayed to the Lord every day to take away her sufferin'. Some days he would listen and the pain would ease, but like those days got less and less.

One of her church friends said that she suffered because she had bad spirits inside her. They said that for a fee they could arrange for a special priest to carry out an exorcism to remove the spirits.

Like, I don't believe in all of that stupidness. Mama was ill, she had MS. The only badness was KJ and his gangsta friends. I told them to leave Mama alone and stopped asking them for any more help. Like, couldn't they see she had enough to deal with without their voodoo stupidness?

Silent Voices

It was just after Halloween; I remember it well, 'cos I had just had a few days off and was working night shifts. It was early evening and I was just leaving for work. Patience rang me to say KJ had been shot; he was in the hospital in Camberwell. She was crying loads and she sounded real frightened. She said could I meet her at the hospital but I said I had work and there would be like nothing for us to do. I told her to text me as soon as she knew what was going on.

I didn't tell Mama. Why? Well she had enough hurt to deal with then. I didn't think that she would be strong enough. I suppose I also thought that KJ wouldn't want her to know. Despite all of the pain he caused her I think he still loved Mama and I don't think he would want her to worry. Lord he had vexed her enough over the years.

Turns out KJ wasn't hurt so bad. Patience texted me lots of times to say he had been in surgery and he was stable. He was being operated on the following day.

KJ was in hospital for over a week. Mama would ask where he was but Patience and I told her he was stayin' with friends. It was best she didn't know.

Patience visited him every day after work and I went with her once. He didn't say much. I think he talked to Patience a lot more when they were alone, but the three of us was a bad recipe.

Some of his gangsta friends put out a YouTube tribute to KJ. I didn't see it and don't rightly know what it said, but I was real mad when I heard about it. Like KJ needed any more publicity to swell his big head. I told Patience to cuss him out over it, but I don't think she ever did.

Anyways we held a family meeting - me, Patience and Mama. It was the day before KJ was due to be sent home. Patience said we had to do it 'cos Mama would know KJ was hurt the moment he set foot in the house. He was on crutches and the doctors said his leg was like permanently damaged, like he would always have a disability with it. He told Patience that the bullet had gone down through his knee cap into his tibia. KJ would need to be an outpatient and attend clinic every week for like a month. He might need further surgery.

Patience and I didn't tell Mama everything. We said KJ had been hit by a motorbike. Like we thought KJ didn't want Mama to know he'd been shot. So we did what we did 'cos it was for the best. No need to make the pain reign. We told her that he would be coming home and then we talked about what we needed to do to get KJ to shape up.

Mama always wanted the best for KJ. She talked about how we needed to understand him more and help him find what he was good at. Me, I just wanted to get on his case like 24/7 - be on top of him so he couldn't breathe without us knowin'. I wanted us to be on him, me or Patience, to keep him wrapped up. Patience said he could stay with her Friday to Sunday and then at the house during the week under lock down. We figured that if we could do it while his leg was still bad, then like we had a chance of turning him round.

Mama hit us with another idea. She said we should find Dada and try and get him back on the scene. I wasn't so sure, like KJ needed another loser male in his life. He had enough of those with his like, loser gangsta friends.

When KJ came back we moved on him. It was subtle at first; lots of sympathy and care. Mama and Patience made all the right moves. For a few weeks it was workin'. KJ started talking sense about finding his own place, a way out, and getting a driving job. I didn't even know he could drive! He even went to church once with Patience and her man. Like Mama was real pleased and took it as a sign that he was knuckling down.

I don't rightly know how Patience did it, but one afternoon she came round with a man I hardly recognised; it was Dada. I was just home from work so we were all there. I don't really know what happened or what was said, but I know Dada didn't stay so long. I suppose KJ didn't say much 'cos it was real quiet when Dada went up to see him. All I heard was the door opening and Dada sayin', "How's my little man?"

Anyways, the moment Dada left KJ lost it. He like busted up his room. Like really busted it up! Smashed everything - furniture, the door, he even punched holes in the walls. Mama started screaming and then the police turned up. Suppose one of them nosy neighbours in the street called them.

We never did repair his room. After that day KJ refused to do anything. He stayed in his room and when he did go out it was only to buy skunk and meet with Samuel. All over Christmas he was like that. That boy was like real tryin'.

As his leg got better he would start stayin' out late and then he was back to his old ways again, only this time he was even more paranoid than before. He hated it when people came to the door, and would never answer it. He never drew open his curtains in his room and only sat in with Mama if the blinds were down. He seemed to take taxis everywhere, other than like when Samuel turned up and they drove off together. Samuel never seemed to have the same car. I don't know how or why. Patience and her man couldn't even afford a car and they were like both earning real money.

My nursing was going real well. The studies were hard but I had the motivation inside me; motivation and a strong dose of faith. That comes from Mama and my faith in the Lord. I always thought that if KJ took time to talk to God he would like find the right path, but he was too busy; busy looking after himself. For KJ it was all about the here and now, and what he could get for himself. I suppose I used to think that if I succeeded and Patience succeeded, like some of it would rub off on KJ.

That all changed one morning in May when the police crashed through our front door and arrested him for attempted murder.

Yes, I knew about the shootin'. It was some gangsta boy from Peckham. I suppose at the time I didn't really pay that much attention. Like, it's just not my world and these boys are always endin' up in some bust up or other over drugs, or money, or girls. I didn't think that KJ would be like stupid enough to be involved in that kinda madness. Anyway the police came and took KJ away in handcuffs. All the neighbours came out to see what was goin' on.

The shame it brought on our family. Mama was crying and screaming not to take her boy away. When they left she collapsed. I like called an ambulance she was in such a bad way. I stayed with her in the hospital all day and all night.

They didn't release KJ. Patience got him a lawyer and visited him. It wasn't easy 'cos he was like in a prison in Feltham. Seems he wasn't the only one arrested. That's why he was like, so far. They didn't want them mixing in the same prison.

The police interviewed us. I didn't mind. I told them what KJ was like and his friends. They were doing their job. Like nursing, it's not easy, but you have to respect anyone who is willing to put on a uniform and go out every day to do a job, helping other people. Yeah, I respect the police, of course I do. If it wasn't for the police like none of us would be safe, right?

KJ was on remand for a long, long time. Mama wasn't well enough to visit him. Then in the summer she got real ill. She had bad times before but this time she got real ill. They took her to hospital and into intensive care. It was the worst of times for me and Patience. Mama didn't recognise us. They put her on a drip and monitors. I tried to be strong for Mama's sake. When I wasn't at work I was at the hospital or I stayed at Patience's. I couldn't be in the house on my own. All I really remember doing was prayin' and cryin', cryin' and prayin'.

A month or so later Mama got released to a hospice down in Dulwich. Two weeks later she died.

I don't remember a darker day.

I'm real sorry but I don't know if I can talk about it anymore. Sorry.

We buried Mama in Nunhead Cemetery. It was a cold wet Friday in September. There were members of the church there and some of Mama's old friends. Patience and I held each other real tight and her man was there taking care of us. It was strange but despite the deep, deep grief and all of the cryin' that day, I remember feeling like this strength around the three of us. It was like Mama was standing next to god with her big arms wrapped around us keeping us save.

I know Patience felt it too - she told me later at the wake.

KJ was there. He was allowed to attend the funeral. He had two guards with him. He was just there for the service and the burial and then was taken away. It's a shame he couldn't stay longer and we could have talked a little. Mama would have liked that.

KJ's trial was in November. It wasn't easy getting to the trials, like what with work and sorting out Mama's things and the house.

Yeah, KJ's trial. Patience and I thought it would be over in a couple of weeks, but it went on for like ever. When I saw KJ in the dock I didn't rightly recognise him at first. He was leaner, but like somehow stronger, determined, like he had power running through his veins. He didn't look frightened; his eyes were dark and powerful, and he never looked to the gallery. All the other boys did but he never once looked for us. I don't rightly know even why we went, but we both knew that mama would expect it of us. Like she would be looking down and telling us hard if we didn't go.

His look never changed. Every time Patience or I went it was the same like throughout the whole trial. He was the only one of the people in the dock whose look never changed. There was an older boy; I don't know him, who looked like life was taken out of him. He was real scared. Samuel was there, struttin' like some bird of paradise. That's until the verdict.

KJ got sentenced to 15 years. I wasn't there on the day but like Patience said, he showed no emotion when the judge passed sentence. 15 years. Lord, that's a long time, but Patience said he would be released before 10 years had passed by.

We visit KJ from time to time. It used to be more but he didn't say much, and to be honest I guess he wanted to just get on servin' his time. He spent some time on the hospital wing like, getting counselling. Appears from what Patience has said that he had a breakdown. Guess what he did to that boy like finally hit home. I'm planning to go and see him again real soon.

I decided to move from the house. It was too full of sad thoughts about Mama and like I felt I wanted a new start, with my own place. But it wasn't easy. Eventually I got the housing association to offer me a new house in North London. Like, it was only one bedroom but it was new and it was mine. I could shut the door and leave the whole world outside. I didn't take anything from the old place, apart from some electricals, pictures and like loads of photographs. They help me remember all of the good times.

KJ's stuff? I bagged it up and shipped it out. I supposed KJ wouldn't be needin' it anymore, and by the time he came out they would all look well old. Anyways, there was like no way I could carry his baggage with me all of my days.

I still go to church and I pray every day to keep my family safe. I have been steppin' out with this man from the church; he's like real respectable and his family are good people. Patience comes with me regular to church. She's planning her wedding for the summer and seeing her so happy is like the best feelin'.

Silent Voices

I visit Mama's grave; me and Patience go regularly. We take flowers and like spend time tidying the grave at least once a month. It's just a little something to show our respect for how much love she gave us and like how much we still love her.

Mama still shines a light on our lives.

What do I think of KJ? I don't rightly know. Like, he had so much goin' for him when he was young. We gave him everything he needed - a warm home, food on the table, the clothes on his back, a loving family. Like, everything we had, he had.

I know you might be thinking we've come down hard on him at times but like, it was out of love for him, to try and keep him on the right path. Do you get it? Otherwise Lord knows, he could have been dead right now.

He knew we all loved him, but sometimes love just isn't enough for some people, is it?

Chapter 5
A Teacher's Story

Thank you for interviewing me. I don't often get to talk to people about my role as a teacher. I mean, I do talk about teaching, but not like this, not in terms of my pastoral role. It's really quite refreshing.

Yes I knew Anton quite well. Well, very well really. He and Timi were quite a pair; not the usual students that we have to deal with, for lots of different reasons.

But yes thank you, let me start with the school and that might give you a bit of context about the challenges that we face, and of course the successes that we have amongst our students.

We like to think of Kingsdale as a bit of an island, a place where our students can learn and grow in a safe environment; a family really, looking after one another, but also somewhere where our students can achieve academically. "Inspiring young people to aspire" is our motto and is something that we constantly remind everyone in the family of our school.

I think that's why we do so well in terms of academic attainment levels. We constantly out-perform similar inner London secondary educational establishments in terms of GCSE and A level grades. Our best performing students are fast tracked so that they can attain the academic qualifications that will lead them onto university and raise their employment aspirations. Some students clearly struggle with the demands, but we have to remember that educational attainment can create an environment of healthy competition, and experience shows that this competition amongst students inspires the majority to higher achievement.

For those that really struggle, we provide alternative opportunities through vocational courses which provide practical skills, tailored for specific career pathways. Resistant materials and construction technology are both very popular courses at the school.

When I first qualified as a teacher, I anticipated a placement in a more suburban school. I had been brought up in a place called Cherry Hinton which is just on the southern outskirts of Cambridge. It's typical middle England I suppose.

Cherry Hinton was once a village but as the university expanded it got swallowed up. It's a really nice place, you know, nothing exceptional, nothing that makes it stand out as a place; just comfortable and safe. We lived in a three bed semi in Greystoke Road. We never moved. My dad was an electrician and my mum was a primary school teacher.

I have one brother, Sean, who still lives in Cambridge and works in the Science Park as a laboratory technician. We had a normal upbringing. We got on pretty well. He is two years older than me and we used to go to school together and he would always look out for me. There was a big park opposite our road called Cherry Hinton Hall, and in the summer we used to play over there all day sometimes. There was an annual folk festival which we used to gate crash; full of hippies and the great unwashed. The music was great though, although I've forgotten it now. What I do remember was the smell of joss sticks that seemed to permeate the air, the distinctive aroma of sandalwood and rosewood intermingled on the warm summer breeze. It was magical.

I bought some joss sticks when I was about 13 and going through my indie-retro- Woodstock phase. I had them burning in my room for hours. It was the only time my dad really lost it with me; told me they were for drug users and threw open every window in the house. Mum and Dad sat me and Sean down that evening and explained why he had acted that way and why drugs were his biggest fear for us. He told us how a friend of his had died in the 70s after taking some bad heroin. He told us how drugs affected you and what would happen if you got addicted.

It really scared us, in a good way, if you know what I mean? What I always remember was the articulate, intellectual way that he described it all. I remember feeling really proud of my dad for treating us so maturely, when what I thought he would do was rant at us.

I went to a really good secondary school called St Bede's. I wasn't a problem pupil, just got on with my work, my homework and got good grades; nothing remarkable but good. I suppose looking back, it all seems really dull, but at the time I just enjoyed life. I had good friends and every Saturday we would take the bus into Cambridge town centre and just hang around the Grafton Centre, or go to the cinema, or sit out on Parker's Piece.

I went to Long Road Sixth Form College and took A-Levels in English, French and History. I had already decided back then that I wanted to be a teacher. I had some good teachers at St Bede's who seemed to have time for us, and even if there were little things that I was worried about, they had an uncanny knack of picking up on it. It probably helped that there were only 24 of us to a class; a number I can only dream of now.

My real passion for teaching was my mum. Every time I went out with her to her school, to help on a parents' evening or school fete, I could see just how much she loved her pupils and how much they loved her. They would crowd around her like moths to a flame, just wanting her attention, offering help with this and that, clumsy fingers which were more trouble than they were worth. But mum just took it all in her stride and somehow everything always worked out.

We had an amazing school prom in the last term, which was the big highlight. Everyone went. Dad bought me a ball gown, which I've still got somewhere at home all boxed up.

The prom was the first time I really got drunk. It was also the first time that I got offered drugs. My friend Harry had some. I didn't really know what he was offering me at first. My parents' talk, all those years ago, had seriously done its job, but some of my friends did and I remember being really shocked. I didn't even know how they could get drugs, let alone take them. They were pills, not coke or anything like that. I think if I had seen my friends snorting coke it would have really freaked me out. One of my friends, Tamsin, took some, and went off with Harry and that was the last I saw of them that night.

The next day I had my first hangover. It's a rite of passage I suppose; an insignificant event in the journey of adolescence. But despite the fact that my parents where ultra-cool about it, all I remember was that it felt anything other than insignificant. Even to this day, I cannot recall ever feeling worse in my whole life. The throwing up was bad enough, but when the room had spun round for the thousandth time, I just wanted to die.

Of course, once I got to university getting drunk was no longer a rite of passage but an essential pastime. I had passed my A-Levels and had been accepted at Bath University, an idyllic setting in the grounds of a former country park between Bath and Bristol. If the step between school and sixth form was a breeze, the move to a university, 300 miles away from home was like a seismic tremor in my protected world. It took me 6 months to settle in and another 2 months to establish some true friends. I worked hard, but the pangs of homesickness affected my concentration, so rather than almost failing through social overindulgence, I nearly failed because of my feeling of social unacceptability. Funny, how the world revolves around our perceptions of how we are seen by others. It resonates so much in terms of Anton and Timi.

The second year, my small band of friends and I rented a converted house on the outskirts of Bath. After that my university life changed. The bond we had of supporting each other was just what I was missing. They become my surrogate family and we looked out for each other and looked after each other. Suzie and I were doing a teaching course, Andrea a degree in History of Art, and Evie a combined English and Philosophy degree. Over the summer we stayed around and got bar jobs, and in term time we studied and played hard.

We had boyfriends, but nothing serious, except one time when Suzie got heavy with a boy called Angus. He was studying law at Imperial College London and used to come down at weekends. I didn't think much of Angus. He was always incredibly arrogant and patronising. Anyway the relationship last about 6 months, then something happened and Angus stopped it dead. Someone said it was something to do with some drugs issue that Angus has got involved in, but all I know was Suzie seemed more relieved than devastated.

Despite the fact that we have all gone in different directions, my flat mates at university have remained my closest friends. We are constantly in contact and meet at least 4 times every year; usually at some dodgy restaurant for lunch or dinner. Andrea got married last year and the four of us went on a luxury, self-indulgent, pampering weekend in a country health resort. It took all of 30 seconds for us to spark up the bond we had in uni, and I don't ever remember laughing so much, for so long.

My course was four years and included the educational teaching qualification that I needed to start my career. Each year we were required to spend a term in a local school. It was an amazing experience, and very daunting. I did 2 terms in primary school and one term in a secondary school, with years 7 and 8. It was like being in the back seat, watching and observing, trying to understand how to use some of the theories like attachment, in a real classroom setting. I even took on the assistant teacher role in the last year for English for a year 7 group, which tested my fortitude and resilience. In year four I spent a lot of time in a placement in a local secondary school and was even allowed work experience teaching lessons. I helped lesson planning and formatting learning programmes to fit the syllabus. I was so stressed out that I would get it wrong, that I hardly slept. Looking back it just makes me smile to remember how I used to be in those early days.

I qualified in 2007. I was applying earnestly for jobs in the home counties or suburban secondary schools. But despite interviews and assessment tests, I never seemed to be lucky. By the time the new academic year had started, I was beginning to really worry. I had spent my whole adolescent life working towards the point of becoming a teacher, and now here I was, back home with no money and no job. I began to think that the world was conspiring against me; a natural, but slightly paranoid reaction. I started applying for jobs as a supply teacher, in the hope that once I get into a school, the chances of a more permanent post would be open to me.

Eventually I got offered a post as a supply teacher at a school in Camberwell, south London. It was called St Michael's and All Angels and I went down for the interview just before Christmas. The nearest tube was Elephant and Castle, and taking the bus down the Walworth Road was like watching an unfamiliar world unfold before my eyes. I wasn't ignorant to the multiculturalism that existed in our urban towns, but what hit me was the ingrained tired shabbiness of what I had always thought of as one of the western world's foremost cities. The street and the buildings looked tired and the grime looked like it had penetrated every pore. The forlorn, almost dejected appearance was reflected in the faces of the people, whose look and demeanour was of subjection; an appearance that I have realised over the last four years is for some, a reality, not just a perception.

The last part of my journey was a five minute walk along Wyndham Road to the entrance of the imposing and overbearing school. Built at the beginning of the last century, it gave the appearance of an outdated institution rather than a centre for learning. The school was surrounded by high rise blocks of flats from the neighbouring Castlemead Estate, and more distant Brandon Estates that seemed to bear down on it like sentinels.

My interview was at 11am and lasted 45 minutes. I was offered the post there and then and asked to start on the 4th January, when the new term commenced. I was given a year 8 form, but also asked to take over English classes, which were a mixture of year 8 and 9 lessons.

Looking back, my 18 months at St Michael's and All Angels gave me the fortitude and resilience to be the teacher that I am now. At the time, however, it was the worst experience of my life. I took a room in a flat share near the Oval, just behind the Myatts Field Estate - mistake number one. I tried really hard to be available to my form class, to offer help and support for their emotional issues as well as their scholastic ones - mistake number two. I tried really hard to make friends amongst my colleagues and build up some close allies, even helping to run a drama group - mistake number three.

What I hadn't realised was that St Michael's and All Angels was a school under siege. It had just become an Academy with a new principle and new senior management team. It was under the spotlight of its funders, and the local authority, following an autumn of unprecedented violence in and around the school. It was under siege from the police and the council, who sent an army of uniformed officers - including mounted police - to patrol outside of the gates at the end of every school day. It was under siege by the parents who believed the school was failing their children and the behavioural issues were a byproduct of poor academic standards, delivered by poor teachers who didn't care. It was under siege by some of the staff who, through passive resistance, opposed the new regime and took every opportunity to undermine it.

But worse of all it was under siege from its pupils and some of its ex-pupils, fuelled by the fact that around 40% of its students came from the Brixton side of Camberwell and 40% from the Peckham side of Camberwell. The other 20% were from every corner of Southwark, caught in the middle of a war that seemed solely based on where a person lived.

I knew none of this on my fist day, but by the end of my first term I was acutely aware and ready to quit. It didn't take long for the students to find out where I lived. They saw me on the bus each day, or walking along Camberwell Road. I was taken as a champion by some and immediately despised by others. The highlight was one year 11 boy who told me he raped girls from 'GAS'; a reference to a rival Brixton gang. I reported it to the school police officer; another concept totally beyond my comprehension; that a school would need its own police officer!

He laughed at the comment and said that the boy was just testing me.

Having opened my door of support, I was flooded with pupils from my form, who off loaded a catalogue of some of the most traumatic, emotional tales of broken families, physical assaults, violent bullying, drug dealers who pressed them into dealing and gang intimidation. I went from disbelief to anger to despair as I tried to resolve the issues, mostly under the strictest instructions of the pupils not to tell their parents or worse, the police. Having tried and failed to make a difference in virtually every case, I then became another let down in their eyes, one of a long line of let downs.

The drama group turned out to be a mini clique of the disaffected teachers, and my desire to establish some friends was overshadowed by the internal school politics. As I tried to add some balance and perspective with other colleagues, I was seen as being disloyal; a snitch by those in the drama clique, and by the Easter break I was cast out.

Finally, just before Easter a pupil was stabbed in the school. The victim wasn't badly hurt but the atmosphere became worse. There was a dark mood over the place. It felt like the school had fallen into a deeper depression, paranoid of what the next move would be and everyone suspicious of everyone else.

The culprit was a boy called Tunde Ojafutu. He was a year 11 student, whose reputation for being violent and aggressive was rife. He had threatened teachers in the past and was regularly met at the end of the school day by older boys, quite often in cars. His younger brother Samuel was in one of my year 8 English classes, a bit cocky but on the whole a nice, bright young boy.

The stabbing wasn't reported in the press. The police officer hushed it up, for the good of the reputation of the school, more than anything else. But it got out eventually and when it did we were descended upon by the council, youth offending service, educational welfare and police investigators. The victim was moved and Tunde permanently excluded. I think he went to a pupil referral unit, but I not entirely sure. There was a rumour that Tunde himself was stabbed in retaliation, but that might have just been a rumour and rumours were rife around St Michael's.

I went home for Easter and very nearly didn't come back. It was Suzie who gave me the determination to succeed. We met up over the break and I broke down in front of her. She told me of her experience during the first term at her school in Nottingham. The similarities were uncanny, although without the same depth of internal politics. Suzie being Suzie, she sat with me and worked out a detailed action plan and personal schedule for the rest of the year. It wasn't just about the school but more about my goals and ambitions; a road map to my next destination.

The road map included moving flat to somewhere away from the school catchment area, joining a gym or a sports club so I had some physical outlet, and finding a kindred spirit - a mentor from another school or area who I could lean on. To be honest the first two were easy. I was always good at the practicalities of life. By the end of the summer I had found a nice flat share in a lovely Victorian house in Lordship Lane, East Dulwich - a rather trendy area full of niche shops and nice cafes. I had played hockey at school and found a club that played in Battersea Park called the Wanderers. They were more social than exceptional, which is just what I needed, and as I rediscovered my latent talent I also discovered that I had a close friendship with one of the players. His name was Alex and by the time I moved we were at the beginning of a relationship. Much to my surprise we are still together.

The mentor happened entirely by chance. I went on a day conference for local school teachers on safeguarding, run by the local authority. It was one of those must do events and took place at Millwall Football Club which I found rather ironic. Anyway I was on a table and started talking to a woman who was a pastoral care teacher at the Globe Academy in Elephant and Castle. Her name was Natalie and within 5 minutes I realised I had found my mentor.

Her passion for her job and her connection with her pupils just shone from her. She had a gravitas about her that I could see wasn't artificial, but a reflection of a self determination to make a difference at whatever cost. I arranged to meet with her for dinner the next week and from there she became by mentor. Natalie reconnected me with my inner self, that part of me that originated my drive to be a teacher, and thanks to her I have been able to make that reconnection every time I face a challenge.

When the new academic year started I was steeled for the term ahead, but I knew ultimately St Michael's wasn't the school for me. I was ready to handle the pupils, but I couldn't manage the school politics, and the constant battle to prove that the approach of some sections of the staff was better than the management. Somewhere the pupils got lost in the middle.

I applied for a job at Kingsdale in the spring. It was for the start of the new academic year. Natalie helped me with the application and even coached me on interview techniques; key buzz phrases that would earn extra marks. I got the job and started in the autumn of 2009.

Kingsdale was totally different. The whole philosophy of the school was different. Inspiration and aspiration were the buzz words, and that was as much for the staff as it was for the pupils. The Principal had been at the school for a long time and had stamped his authority in every class room, corridor and paving slab. The reputation of Kingsdale meant everything, and that was distilled in the pupils and staff alike. That reputation of a high achieving school was as much about what we did outside of the school gates as inside the school and if anyone brought the reputation of the school into dispute, they were swiftly dealt with.

There was also no school police officer, not because the principal disliked police but because he fervently believed that it was up to the staff and pupils to police the school; a doctrine that was readily accepted by the majority. Don't get me wrong, there are just as many troubled young people in Kingsdale as at St Michael's. The school is based as far south on Southwark as you can be, with the boundaries of Lambeth and Bromley only a few hundred metres away, and Croydon and Lewisham not much further away. There are pupils from different areas that attend the school, but the rivalries don't exist in the same way as they did in St Michael's. Of course there have been incidents. It was that September in 2009 that Samantha Joseph, Danny McLean and a number of other boys were convicted of Shakilus Townsend's murder. There was a strong connection for the pupils and those involved, and the nerves were still raw. But somehow the murder strengthened the ethos of the school, and despite Shakilus's faults, he was aspiring to do better. We put on counselling support and I was asked to co-ordinate both this and the aspects of pastoral care.

In met Anton, Timi and KJ in my first year. They were in their first year of A-Levels. I didn't teach them but I got to know all three through my pastoral role.

What did I think of them? Well, Anton and Timi were certainly characters. Both were very bright, Timi was more articulate, I supposed very self-opinionated. Both used their intellect and well-honed charm to try and illicit as much out of everything and everyone that they came across. Anton didn't have the charisma of Timi and there was something rather emotionally immature and vindictive about him. He wanted to please everyone, to be obsequiously charming - probably a trait that came from his home life. I think it also came from his constant attempts to intellectually and emotionally out manoeuvre Timi.

Timi was the real powerhouse of the three; he clearly had a goal. Studying politics, sociology and economics, gives you an idea of the kind of ambitions that he had. But Timi liked to play psychological games, I could see it in the way he manipulated his friends, but I also experienced it first hand in one of my pastoral support sessions. It was like he was actually assessing me, testing for my intellectual and personal weak points, finding which buttons he could push; not immediately, but saved for that special occasion in the future when he needed it. It wasn't until half way through one session that it dawned on me that I was talking about how my time in St Michael's had affected me, something that I regretted when he consistently asked me how I was and he "hoped the pressure at the school wasn't affecting me".

I was so furious with myself for allowing my guard to drop. I talked to Natalie about it, hoping for some empathy; it didn't come, but what I did get was a real reality check. Natalie told me that for people like Timi, their street survival was wholly based on his ability to intellectually out manoeuvre other members of his group, younger and older. Where some of his friends could use their connections or family members to build their reputation, others could use their emotional detachment to carry out violence to sickening degrees. She told me of Timi's street rep; Timi was the brains, spending his whole life like he was playing chess, always thinking ahead and keeping that one move away from trouble.

KJ was a different proposition entirely. It wasn't until I spoke to Natalie that I realised just how much sympathy I had for him. I could never quite put my finger on what it was about KJ, but I could clearly see that he was desperately searching for something that always seemed to be just out of his grasp. If I had to put it into one word I would say that it was acceptance. I am sure it was deeper than just acceptance as an equal with his two friends, Timi and Anton, although from everything I observed, he was manipulated by both of them.

KJ wasn't bright like Timi or Anton but he was good with his hands and was looking to take a vocational course in construction. He seemed in to look up to Timi, like he was his guide - but KJ had a temper and although I never saw him use it towards Timi he did with Anton, on several occasions. You could always tell when Anton pushed it too far, because despite his charm, it was Anton that was the one that got excluded from the trio.

The following autumn, I noticed that KJ wasn't at school. I went to the Principal to try and find out what had happened. He asked me to sit down and in confidence told me that KJ had been shot. He said that the police had informed him and that it was imperative that the news didn't get out and that any gossip was quickly squashed. He asked me what I knew about his friends and I told him all of the fears about Timi and Anton. We agreed to keep a close eye on both boys and we elicited the support of their tutors.

I was also told that KJ wouldn't be coming back to school because of the risk to other pupils. I found that very hard to understand. KJ had been a victim of a shooting and surely we had to show compassion. The Principal reminded about our ethos, and that it was imperative that the duty of care for the rest of the pupils and the reputation of the school were paramount. KJ would be referred to a college which would provide for the vocational courses that he wanted to follow.

Christmas came and went. It was quite memorable for me because it was the first Christmas that Alex and I spent together on our own, no families, no pressure, just us in our own delightful world.

Silent Voices

When I heard Anton had been shot and later died, I was totally shocked. Of course I knew that guns and violence were not uncommon in South London. I'm not that naïve, and the incident with KJ was still raw. But I never thought that someone that I knew personally, someone who I would actually be connected to, would lose their life to gun violence.

The school was in total shock. I mean literally the whole school was in shock. We had special assemblies for the pupils and group support meetings for the staff. Counsellors were brought in to help some of the pupils who were clearly affected. The school took a group of pupils to lay flowers at the spot where he was murdered, and on the day of the funeral we allowed pupils to attend. Over a hundred went, all in school uniform, along with the Principal and the some of the form teachers. I went as well. I can't tell you just how moving it was. I cried throughout the whole service.

I met Anton's mum and his brother, who I hadn't seen before. I didn't really know what to expect, I suppose, but his mum was beside herself with grief. She didn't sob, she wailed - a sound I can never forget. She wailed as if her grief was being ripped right out of her soul. She could hardly stand, and Anton's brother and other members of the family were trying to hold her up. The brother just looked numb, as if he wasn't really there. The intensity of the grief was stifling and I could hardly breathe with the pressure of it.

For the next few weeks, the police were ever present around the school. The Principal was less than happy, but for once even his authority wasn't strong enough to resist. But it didn't take long for them to start to disappear. It took much longer for the school to settle down. In fact it didn't really begin to shake off the impact until very recently.

Some of the pupils asked the Principal if they could hold a music festival in Anton's name, as a way to raise some money for the family to pay for a headstone. I know it sounds really odd to have a festival, but the family wasn't very well off and they couldn't afford a headstone at that time. We held the festival just before the Easter break; it was great, very upbeat and very moving. I think for some of the pupils it was a way of dealing with their grief. We raised over a thousand pounds through ticket sales and auctions on the night. It really helped change the mood, and I'm sure it was a comfort for the family.

One of the more unpleasant aspects that I remember with real clarity was the Facebook messages. There were lots of really positive messages about Anton; how much his life touched others, that the world was a dark place now that Anton's flame had gone out. There was some family stuff as well, very emotional and quite touching.

But I found it very hard to comprehend some of the other messages, which clearly came from some very disturbed people; messages saying he deserved to die, he was a soldier who chose to fight and lost his life; some even celebrated the killing. I can't imagine how the family must have felt when they read them, but it made me feel sick. What depraved human beings could make such comments about a young man? I wondered if some of the students who were walking around me all day, were those who thought that way. Had the world around me become so sick in such a short time, or had I just been oblivious to a disengaged, disingenuous generation who gave the impression of wanting to aspire, when really they just wanted to deceive and get by?

My faith in my students returned, albeit with guarded cynicism, after we had a debate about Facebook in one of my form sessions. We talked about what had been posted about Anton, and my students all expressed their own anger and contempt about the negative remarks that they had seen and read. Interestingly, from my perspective, was that they didn't condemn Facebook, or those that posted the comments., they blamed the police for not policing the sites, parents for not policing their children's use of the sites and de facto, the whole media, for creating an acceptance of violence, almost promoting it as a gritty urban lifestyle.

I thought that the impact of the murder was behind me, well behind us, as a school, when the new academic term started. But the biggest jolt was reading the names of those who were on trial for Anton's murder, seeing Samuel, KJ and Timi's names there. To read Timi's name was surprise but not a shock. After all he was a close friend of Anton. But I never felt he would end up involved in murdering anyone. Getting right in the thick of things just wasn't part of his characteristic, rather he would be orchestrating from a distance.

Hearing KJ's name wasn't a shock, but instead a more resigned disappointment. I never believed that KJ was a bad person, but he kept bad company and was the kind of young man that would be manipulated. I just recall saying to myself that it would be others that would lead him into the ultimate trouble. He was a willing foot shoulder who would act on the word of others with no acknowledgement of the consequences to himself.

No the shock was seeing Samuel named as the murderer. For some reason I just couldn't associate Samuel, that cocky year 8 student from my days at St Michael's, with becoming a killer. I suppose I had, for some unfathomable reason, boxed all of those experiences at St Michael's, separately from all of the connections with Kingsdale.

My naivety hit home again, as I suddenly realised that I segmented my worlds, parcelled them up into neat little packages that fitted in with my life and not the life of those students that I had taken pastoral care for. Why wouldn't Samuel, KJ, Timi and Anton know each other? Kingsdale was a school that prided itself in having an eclectic geographical mix of students, from Peckham, Camberwell, Tulse Hill as well as the immediate area.

What I learnt most from that whole experience was that for the pupils that I had care for, I would never try to detach the world outside of the school from their world in the school. I recently started studying a counselling course on evenings and weekends so that I could improve my ability to offer emotional support. It was Natalie's suggestion, and I have to say it was really comforting, being able to get back into the discipline of studying, using my academic ability so that I could apply it to support others.

Life is all about experiences isn't it? Learning from what is thrown at you and treating it as an opportunity that can help you grow and develop. I really hope this is something that I am able to impart to my students, and provide them some support as they start their journey. It's part of my philosophy and part of the school's philosophy in inspiring others.

For the first time since I left home in Cherry Hinton - that cocooned environment that seems a million miles away from my life in South London - I don't feel that I am striving to find my place in the world. I'm happy in my personal life, but most of all I am happy with my life as a teacher. I'm doing some voluntary work with Natalie as part of her organisation, The Sunday Essiet Company, providing mentoring for young people who are starting out in the adult world. It is very rewarding, being able to use my skills in such a positive way.

Anton's murder was a dark time, but I've learnt a lot from it and know that it's made me a more resilient person. It's something that I can draw some strength from. It has helped reinforce my view that a strong nurturing school environment, which provides a challenging learning experience, is so important to help prepare young people for life ahead of them. Schooling and education is a safe haven from the chaotic world around them and I am privileged in being able to help them on their journey.

Chapter 6
Andre's Story

Yeah yeah man, I don't mind. I'mma gonna talk to you, just chill man I got nothing to hide. What else am I gonna do in here other than talk? Talking's the least of my worries now, trust me. It's not like I'm gonna get into bigger beef from talkin' to man like you, just relax.

So what you wanna know, like I was some kinda big boss man, huh?

Well back in the day I had a street rep yeah, I had some notoriety, real respect man, I won't deny it. But that was back in the day yeah, I've left that life behind long time, trust me. Too much blood on the road, all my boys either dead or inside. I was like the last one, and even then, they got me for doin' something that was right, not even something that was wrong; man that's what hurts the most.

Yeah, so my story. Hope you got some time, we got a lot to talk about. You better sit back and relax, we gonna do some serious reasoning.

I was born in Kingston, Jamaica, in the late 80's. Man it was a time of war on the streets and what my Mama must have thought bringing me into that world, only God knows. I don't rightly remember my dad. Like I don't recall him, like someone who was there for me. I remember him, I remember the last day I saw him like I am breathing it. Dem men burstin' into my daddy's house and slicin' him up.

There must have been a dozen of them, but for all I knows there could have been an army. The noise and the screamin'. My granddaddy tryin' to protect him but they tore him off. He had slice marks on his arm.

My mama was screamin' and holdin' me and Kelvin to protect us. She was trying to cover our eyes but I saw them slicing him; the blood, the screamin'. The noise of those blades from the ratchet knives was so clean like they were slicing air. But the blood man, there was so much blood, splattered their clothes, the walls, the furniture. When I looked down my feet and legs were covered in red blotches. I saw it all. They just kept slicing my daddy up.

They dragged my mama away from us down the street; I thought she was dead. No police came, there was no ambulance man, wot you must be jokin'! This was Trench Town. Down here, we don't call police, dem just as bad. As for the ambulance they don't exist unless you have money to pay on their arrival, so ambulances is for uptown people; dem with money. When the man disappear and the sun set, some neighbours came in, wrapped up daddy and bundled his flesh and bones to the hospital, but it was a waste of a drive; we knew he was dead.

It wasn't until early hours when Mama came back. They had raped and beaten her. There was blood all down her legs and her face was swollen so bad I hardy recognised her. They had cut her face, gave her a telephone cut - that's a slice from ear to mouth. In Jamaica that was the deadliest cut you could give someone if you wanted to leave a mark. My grandma cleaned her up and took her to the clinic. The hospital was for the dyin' man; too many prying eyes and questions for the living. Now the clinic was the place where you saw the real truth of the ghetto; Trench Town back then. Mama never said a word about what had happened, but man, from that day, she stopped being my mama. Mama never held us from that day to the day she died, like she forgot we were her boys and needed her love and protection. She must've been thinking that her pain was too hard to share.

Some men started coming round. She had no choice to do their business, some holdin', some carryin', some other stuff I don't wanna talk to. They gave her crack as payment. First she sold it to pay for food, or bartered it. But I guess the pain of what they did just kept on bearin' down on her. She started takin' some of that shit to cover all dat hurt. Then she was hooked bad.

Yeah I remember real good. I must have been 6 or 7 back then. Kelvin was round 9 or 10 when they butchered daddy. It taught me some deep lessons - kill or be killed - don't put your trust in man; it's all about you, number one. Some of the olders talk of time on the Islands like some paradise. But I seen pain and hurt there dat stick deep man, deep in my throat.

We got sent to Britain, me, Kelvin and mama. We were packed up and shipped out, like we were some rats being cleaned out of the neighbourhood. Not that Kelvin and me minded; it was a big adventure. Granddaddy said that we were going to make a new life in a new home, all clean and safe. I was 11, man I just bought that lie and ate it up.

We arrived and got taken deep into London and put up in a flat in Peckham. It was long back and I was a youngen, but man, I thought my world was on the up. Mama was off the smack. She said that she would get cleaned up and make up the years. Kelvin and I got into schooling at Waverley. We had uniforms like we were some swanky rich kids.

None of it lasted. Mama was sent over by the boys from Kingston. Before long we had men in and out of our door, day and night, and mama was back on the white sugar. The three of us lived in one bedroom in dat flat. Some of the men took over the other bedroom, then the sitting room. They cooked up crack in the kitchen. No man they didn't harm us, you not getting it. They had other, ulterior plans for us. They just bided their time.

We lived out of plastic bags piled high in that one room. The curtains were never opened. Kelvin and I slept on a dirty double mattress, rolled up every morning and rolled out every night. Days went by when we just ate take away food in dat room, did our homework when we had a reason, or just watched TV. Sometimes we listened to music, to cover up the sounds from the rest of the flat; partyin', laughin', screamin' and beatin's. I remember the screamin' most. Dang, that screamin' of deep pain. Took me straight back to that night in Kingston. Man, much of the madness of my days on road in Peckham was to get that screamin' out of my head.

Kelvin and me, well we just weren't ready for school; either that or school just wasn't ready for us. Kelvin tried harder than me. I just beat my way through the first three terms and come the new school year got excluded.

Man I been excluded a long time, just someone forgot to tell me so. For Kelvin his fall was like, real deep man. When his time came to face up, he took it real bad. He robbed a boy in Rye Lane and beat him hard. When he came home he found mama lyin' on the bed, she'd been battered by one of dem men. Kelvin went right out that night and found that piece of shit; beat him so bad, right in front of his woman and child, that he blinded him in one eye.

From that day Kelvin and me hit the road. By the time I was 14 and Kelvin was 17 we were running drugs. Not carrying man, I mean runnin'. It was around 2002 or 2003 and crack was da ting. We got supplied by the olders. Dem men who ran our house, started running us; crack, cheese, heroin from the Turks, man they got it all.

They has us man from day one, right from when we set foot in Peckham; dang even before we left the Islands. We just like a small piece in a big food chain, like we servin' the tills whilst the big man runs the whole company. We started on the front line, but didn't take long for us to move up. We got a rep and we had protection; man soon learnt not to mess with us. You cross us, we dealt with you and if you took us on, the olders stepped in. Boy den you in real trouble, when your name's called you're a dead man walkin'.

Yeah but back in the day crack was where it was at. That stuff messes with your head. We cooked it up, just like the boys did in our house. But we mixed it with a load of shit. We used bi-carb and ammonia most days. But we used anything we could - used caustic soda once. Dat shit burns. Dem crack heads were just a line of cash to us. No one's gonna come back for a refund man, you know what I'm sayin'?

We had a proper posse then. We were the original Peckham Boys, none of that street madness that goes on now. That's just crazy stuff man; boys dyin' on da road for a bag of weed. No, we really ran things; we had Peckham in lock down. There were around ten of us. We didn't put roots down, we kept smart. We had street kids who would do anything for us. They delivered and hit the streets; front line. We set up the houses, ran the money and enforced when we needed. We had rivals from Brixton, PDC boys,

SMS and Ghetto Boys, but we kept things tight, so an incursion was dealt with. If any of the crews really stepped out of line, we enforced hard.

I was strapped by the time I was 15 - nothing fancy - a Glock that had seen time. Getting the weapon wasn't hard but finding ammo was harder. Punished one of the runners who was getting out of line. Nothin' serious, just a cap in his leg. Can't say it did anything for me back then. For me, if I really wanted to punish someone, beatin' them was my ting. But I had to have a strap 'cos a few years later things startin' getting real hot. Some of the boys wanted to start their own ting, muscle in and take over. They started a turf war man, like we never had close time. They set up their own crews, started recuitin', set up Brooklyn, Jarrett and the Gat gang. But me and Kelvin and some of the old crew were on them. Some of them dead, some inside, some long gone. The ones we didn't take out the police did. We punished their youngers just to make sure. Kidnapped one of their brothers, one time, kept him locked up, then returned him the next day with a cap with his name on. He was 8.

It's all about respect man, that's what it's about, respect and money, the big G's. You gotta understand that on the streets, respect is king. You got to demand respect and if you don't get respect you gotta punish hard. We hunted people down over disrespect. We had to break them, 'cos if they think you are soft then you a dead man walkin'. You can tell when a man's gone soft by lookin' in his eyes; you see the spark's gone.

People challenged us. Kelvin got hunted down one time leaving Aristocrats in Camberwell. It was one of our clubs like the RnB in Peckham. But one time, this wannabe was waiting outside for him with a Mac 10. Let off 28 rounds man, but only hit Kelvin twice. He was the cousin of one of the Jarrett boys. We hunted him down, caught him in Clapham; stuck three caps in him. Man on street didn't mess with us.

Yeah that was back in the day. Dem youngers came up on the streets and we gave them our blessing to run the front line. The PYG they called themselves. We let them build an army man - drugs, businesses, music, extortion, counterfeit money, girls; man we ran it hard. We had lots of girls. They were there the whole time, on us, shakin' their booties in front of us. Man we had lots of girls. I never kept a woman, just used them. But I never raped, I drew the line on rape. Kelvin's another story, but not me. The pain of seein' Mama comin' home covered in blood, battered and marked, must have run real deep. Some of the youngers now, man they go too far. If they touched my girl like they do some others, man there would be blood on the streets.

Looking back I know what kept me goin'. Man, when you get time to reflect you can see your whole life mapped out. I demanded respect, but I had no respect. I respected nothin'. I mean life meant nothin'. I could have taken your life while you sat right in front of me, 'cos to me you were nothin'. Do you get me? I owed you nothing and you were worthless. I'd have beaten you for just steppin' on my shadow.

But reflection had told me that I didn't respect man because I never respected myself. Life growin' up in Kingston, with a shell of a women who was my Ma, living in Peckham with people who took everything they could; life told me that I was worth nothin'. If I hurt someone it meant nothin', if I got hurt it was a relief. Pain was like a drug, because physically when I was in pain, I felt somethin'. It reminded me I was alive.

Life had told me to love nothin', so I shut out everythin'. Even when mama died, takin' a big hit after tryin' to stay clean for 6 months, it meant nothin'. It was two years later when I was inside that I finally cried. I work up early in the morning, about two am just cryin' and cryin'. I couldn't stop. I cried for hours. It was the first time since the day my daddy died.

No, back in the day I did things that make me sick lookin' back, like I was someone else. In here I have time to reflect, real deep reflection inside, right to my soul.

The cops were on me all the time. I got stopped and searched so many times I got to know every one of them. They tried to pin me down, charged me with shit, but nothing stuck. No one wanted to be seen to take us on. There were days when them fedz would come down and beat up some of the youngers; pistol whipped one boy right outside his front door. But never me or Kelvin. No we just got shaken down so many times I gave up counting. I finally got time back in 07 - possession; my Glock and a kilo of smack. Got caught running a line to Taunton. Man of all the places to get nicked. I spent my whole life running the streets of Peckham and I get caught in Taunton. Got 5 years and served three. I was 19.

That first time prison was a breeze; that is until I woke up cryin'. Was in Exeter Prison on remand for 6 months, then sent to HMP Verne. Verne is in Dorset. Kelvin came to see me and some of the olders. But it was a long way. There were two of us in a cell, just big enough for the bunks and a small table. The toilet was in a small recess with a curtain round it. Some days spent 23 hours in that cell. There were supposed to be courses and stuff. Often they were cancelled. There was a gym that we were given time to use, but mostly we just had time, lots of time. Food was smuggled in; mostly cheese and some smack. Cheese man, wot you sayin' you never heard of cheese? Cheese man, weed, skunk; man where you been livin'?

Some boys got it rough inside, but not me. I could beat a man real hard, and boy, no one messed with me. Some of the boys were beaten, some of the youngers became the wings' sweet heart. One of the PYG boys got done so hard he ended up in hospital; ripped his rectum right open. Not my scene man and they knew it. Any move against me in dem early days I dealt with real hard. Inside is no different to out. You gotta earn respect. Respect is king.

I got a visitor about 18 months in; one of the girls that hung with us. I knew her real good from back in the day on the streets. She had a little baby with her, about a year or so, I didn't rightly know. She said it was mine, that she would wait for me when I came out. I don't know why, boy I did nothin' to lead her thinkin' that we would hook up. But whatever her motives were, she got inside my head. Lord knows why but next day I went to see the chaplain. I didn't say much, kept it sweet and talked about the girl. Dang that man went and started asked about my mama. He got deep man, first time I talked to him he got deep and it hurt.

Followin' mornin's when I woke up cryin'. That's the mornin' my life started changin'. Lookin' back you know that girl - her name's Marline - she hit me with one blow that broke me down. She hit that one weak spot in that big old wall that I put up and broke it down. I saw the chaplain all days I could and then the psychiatrist. She said something that stuck the knife in, real deep. She said that I'd had an emotional break through, not an emotional breakdown. Man she pressed that button so hard, telling me that for my whole life, since that day daddy died, I was livin' an emotional breakdown, right 'til Marline gonna went and walked through that door, with my baby girl.

Man that caused me some pain, it got me to wise up right there and then, realisin' that I still had time to make things happen. I started studying. Got every book I could and started studying real hard; did a business course. Dem prison guards thought I'd found God, the change was so sudden, but I'd just found myself, dug my soul right out from deep inside me.

The chaplain hooked me up with some people in Camberwell for when I got out - St Giles. Said they would put me on some course and help me get started properly, when I got released. One of their people came up to see me, called Joseph. He was an ex-offender; told me his story, where he was at. It was real easy 'cos for the first time, I was talking to someone who got it, understood all the road shit. When I got out we met, got me hooked up real good.

Best ting in my life, Marline and my little girl. Man, Marline, she has some fight in her, wanting to link up with me. Turns out she was 17 when she found out she was expecting. Her mama got real mad an' kicked her out. She was at college, studying child care or someting - ended up in a hostel in Queens Road. But despite everything life threw at her, she kept on studying, kept the baby, got her own place through housing in some mother and baby place off Havil Street, Peckham. Man she is one resilient girl; knows what she wants and goes right out an' gets it.

Turns out she had her eye on me long time; thought I had some good locked up inside. She remembers it all, the parties we were at, the times we were together. I wrote her. Man I don't recall writin' to anyone in my life. Inside they give you this small pencil and some cheap paper that rips every time you press hard. When your hands are freezing numb, tryin' to write with a bitty pencil is hard, real hard. When I started, I couldn't get down what I wanted. So I just wrote "thank you". Yeah, two words, "thank you". For some reason when I wrote dem words down, shit, it opened up a whole heap of things I wanted to say, I just couldn't stop. Told her tings I never dreamed of tellin' man. All with that stubby pencil and dem scraps of paper.

They transferred me before my release to some lower cat prison - HMP Ford. Not so many lock downs or rules. Marline met me at the gate that last day. Man I knew dat my life changed. I moved in with her - not straight off - I had tings to lay down first. Personal tings man, you get what I'm saying. Tings that would end my former life. I saw Kelvin, told him the new road I was on. He got it; respected me for it. He never stood in my way, but he made sure I knew that I would never shake my rep. Others would come lookin', so I had better be prepared.

Some three months on, I was at Marline's. We lived in that studio flat for long time. The landlord found out and gave us a hard time. Sometimes man makes life real hard.

I hooked up with Joseph, like I said. Got tings sorted, real good. Took me into St Giles and I started doing some work wit' them helpin' man coming out of jail. I finished studying my course and got qualified. Was workin' with St Giles long time; helpin' others off road, feelin' real good. It's the one ting I'm qualified for, the whole road life. Like, I've been living my life to get to this point, to help others.

Refection, that's wot you gotta do; take time to reflect. That's what I been telling them boys, you gotta reflect. Man the truth is that the pain in me ran real deep. I developed hate because inside I was hurtin' real bad and there was no one to help me. I made some bad choices; I did some real crazy tings. But I'm not proud of it; it never healed me, just made it worse.

The whole road ting, it's all a big lie. There's no respect on road, people just fear you and you end fearin' everyone, you get it? You end up fearin' everyone, and truth is you fear who you are and wot you've become. Man its deep but it's the God's truth. You wanna get off road, den you listen; don't go on road.

I told this to some of dem youngers. Boy, they a real hard bunch - KJ, Timi, Darell, Michael, Samuel; yeah man I knew them all. I told them long time. Tink they came to me to get respect, but I told them, "man you want my respect, you stay off road. You wanna go on road, then you got it coming hard". Some of dem listen; some of them just get dragged in. Darell and Michael they listen, but man some of their friends just drag them back in real deep. Samuel, he was just some street punk, real dumb and full of shit. Man he not know it but some of the olders had him marked, and when you're marked you gonna get it, inside or out. He gonna get it rough inside, trust me.

KJ was no gangster, man what you saying? You still don't get street! KJ was just the front man, nothing else, the boy they could set up and take the hits. I talked to KJ long time. I could sense his pain. Every time I saw KJ it was like looking in a mirror. No KJ needed help man, but come my time it was too late. Saw his father once and told him straight; even threatened him if he didn't wise up and help out.

Timi, now Timi was different. I spent long time with Timi, got inside him real good. Timi was smart, man he was smart. He could work any one of that crew, turn over tings and always keep his hands clean. I gave Timi time; helped steer his path. I liked Timi, he gor real style I'm tellin you. Of all does boys, Timi had culture, he goin' places even den. But der was another ting. See Timi protected. In his head he think that he made choices, but he still don't get it. The olders, they protected him, helped him, so that when time come he can start runnin' the business. Even helped set him inside the machine; workin' with those stooges in the council, and the fedz. Man them olders got him wrapped up so tight he can't even see it.

I hardly knew Anton - met him few times with the boys on the front line. I didn't think much of him man, seemed to be leechin' off the other boys, swinging on Timi's tails and pretending to be a big man. I seen boys like that every day, trying to be something big and then seein' they are in too deep. That boy lost some wraps one time. It was KJ's food that I'd given him - nothing big; £20 bag of cheese. But he gone and got busted with it. So come pay day - KJ couldn't deliver - the debt went to £200. Man that boy Anton so stupid, he tried to hide out. KJ knew the score; if he didn't clean it up, I would have to deal with him. It's respect man, he knew the rules of the road. Dem boys paid up, but from that day Anton was marked.

But you listen good. Timi had nothing to do with Anton's killin'. Don't you go listen to dem Fedz, I'm tellin' you, dey full of shit man. They wanna pin shit on Timi for long time, cos he too smart for dem. Timi was no where near dat scene dat night, I'm tellin' you. I know where Timi was, but I'm not tellin' da Fedz nothin'.

I kept clean, real clean. Yeah I ran a few errands now and then. Nothing heavy, but you can't turn your back on your Bredrin straight off. But Marline and my girl were my life; they are my one big ting. Man I was so off road, I could see life laid out in front of me. Marline got a part time job in a care home - done real good, I'm proud of her. Days she was workin' I took my little girl to school, or picked her up. Man I miss her real bad, miss seen' her and listenin' to her read to me every day.

Boy, I been stupid, I'm mean, real stupid. One time I got back in, dragged in, just one time and look at me now. You tell those kids not to get on road, you get me?

Two of the boys came to me that night, the night Anton got capped. They had the strap with them; wanted me to deal with it. I told them to keep me out of it, told them they were dumb. Then I got a call from one of the olders, made my choices clear. So I got the boys to wrap it good so I didn't touch it. Hid it in da bin chute. Moved that dam strap every day. Suppose man must have seen me stashing it in the drain pipe, 'cos the fedz turned up and arrested me. Seems they'd been tailing me; work of some snitch. I knew I was done, moment they turned up. Took me off. Dang, never even had time to call my girl. Missed the school pick up. They never even cared.

Man, I made one bad move, dang ruined me, right there and then. I lost everythin'; all that time, all those years on road demandin' respect. You know dat road respects no man - it's a dead end. I went on road and lost everythin. Even one time I tried to keep off road, it dragged me down and spat me out. One dumb move. Road demanded one more dumb move. Truth is dem olders made my choice clear - if I didn't do it, they were gonna rape my girl. I couldn't do that to her. They knew me, inside an' out. Just couldn't see Marline goin' through what my mama went through.

So I'm servin' a long 9. Probably be out in 5. But shit, this time it's real hard. I miss my girl real bad. I miss my little baby. Marline's not bin long time. She wrote to say she moving away. Boy that hurt so bad. But I get it, I ain't there to protect her and she's never been on the whole road ting. Man I lost everythin'. I'll make it up to her - die tryin' - but I just want my life back. Thrown it all away man. I got my whole life on track and they ripped it right out from me. I can't tell you how hard the pain hurts; not the pain like gettin' a beatin'. Dis pain is deep, deep inside me, right in my soul; hurts so bad I can't breathe. Man I don't know if I can do time no more. I just need to get out and get my girl back. I don't want my little girl growing up seein' me as some road man. I want her to be proud of me; give her some respect.

Joseph's moved on. Got some new face linked with me. Said he'd come down to see me, but it's been months. You know all these people come and go; they just drop me and move on - just another long line of people who want the credit and then leaving me, like I never even existed to them. They just want the headlines; stand up in front of government and say "look we're great", when the truth is I'm sitting in here with shit.

You're the same. I talk to you, give you all this shit and you'll be long gone. Man, my girl Marline and my baby were the only ones who stuck it through.

Kelvin? Kelvin's long gone! He's dust man. Went back to Jamaica - told him straight he would be a dead man walkin'. He's dust; long time.

Yeah, you can tell my story. But you make sure you tell it straight. Man took everything from me, ripped me up. My life's been ripped up long time. Road's done nothing. Whatever I had, road's taken it away.

Just wanna get my life back; want my girl back. I know it's gonna be hard. But I know what I gotta do - earn her respect, prove I'm a real man she can trust and rely on. I gonna do what it takes, gonna prove it to her, make her proud of me, like I'm proud of her. I owe it to her you know. If it takes a lifetime to find her I'm gonna do it, protect her real good, like my daddy wanted to do but couldn't. Life can give you some bad cards but it's how you play them that makes the difference.

Just wait till I get out of here, you know what I'm saying, I just need to get out of here.

Chapter 7
It's A Cultural Thing

―――――――――――――

The second dynamic factor is culture. Culture is more than the class, family, ethnic or religious backgrounds of people. Although the characters described perceive the world through different lenses, those lenses have already been created by much wider cultural influences.

Understanding the various aspects of culture gives us the opportunity to start influencing them, so that the perceptions that Anton, his family, Timi and the other characters set out in these pages have are not the cultural norms for another generation.

Peckham, and the neighbouring area of Nunhead - which make up the areas surrounding Rye Lane - have a defined culture. But its current culture is by no means as established and historical as you might think. The 7 square kilometres area which makes up the 5 wards of Peckham and Nunhead represents around one quarter of the London Borough of Southwark. There are around 72,000 residents, which again represents about a quarter of the borough's overall population. However, young people up to the age of 19 who live in this tight, dense area, make up nearly a third of the whole borough's youth population.

Peckham, or key parts of Peckham, are described as areas of high deprivation. 50% of residents live in social housing and 40% live below the average household income level. 7.2% are unemployed and receive some form of state benefits. The average life expectancy is around 75 years-10% lower than other areas of the borough. The average across London is 80, and for the United Kingdom it is closer to 86. There are significant health related problems which exist including, chronic terminal illness such as cancer, diabetes, mental ill heath, sexually transmitted diseases, drug and alcohol dependency.

The ethnic diversity of its residents is stark. Almost 40% of the population are described as being from black ethnic backgrounds, with 20% black African, 10% black Caribbean, and a further 6% from other black ethnic groups. Combined, these figures are 10% higher than the rest of the borough.

There are 500 hundred churches stretched across Southwark, representing every possible domination. In Peckham, black evangelical and Pentecostal churches dominate the area and dominate family life. The passion for God's love and protection is of primary importance, although you might be forgiven for thinking that the costs - charged by a small handful of ministers for the privilege of praying in God's church - outweigh the benefits.

Churches can be found in abandoned bingo halls; on semi used industrial estates; in offices closed at the weekend; or low cost community halls. Religion matters, as it helps to shape what humanity should look like as opposed to the reality of what it really looks like in the lives of the congregation. Life is hard and sometimes very lonely when your immediate neighbours have little time for neighbourly support. So the church is a small island where faith unites cultures for a few hours, a few times a week.

Meanwhile in some of the more hidden and darker reaches, ministers carry out spiritual exorcisms to remove the bad spirits that have taken over a person's soul. Voodoo exists and dominates some peoples' lives. It is used as a threat - a dark magic that can be inflicted on a person - and for those influenced by it, is as real as the hand in front of their face.

Religion, faith and religious beliefs are as much a part of today's culture as they were over 150 years ago. Just as the diversity of what makes up Peckham today will change, so will the make-up of religion. Faith, in its truest meaning will always remain, even if it is sometimes blind to the real pressures that exist inside families and the traumatic experiences that they have to endure every day.

Peckham is like a sponge; absorbing people from a diverse range of backgrounds - many, but not exclusively - with high dependency, whilst at the same time wringing out the more socially mobile.

But the actual culture of Peckham is not what is visible today. Peckham has not always been an area of deprivation, and its demographics of today are not the demographics of a decade ago, the decade before that, or the decade ahead of us. Still, the inherent culture of Peckham remains; the same culture that existed when Peckham and Peckham Rye was an affluent location - 'the place to be', in the late 19th Century.

The culture of Peckham is the very fact that it is and always will be the starting point of a social journey. It is a foothold for those who are trying to establish a place in life; or the first step towards a different life; or the chance to stop slipping into a spiral of life dependency.

And the reason why people stay in Peckham is less to do with being 'stuck', and more to do with sticking; sticking with the support they get, from services, friends families, neighbours, their church, or sticking with the vibrancy, colour and life of the place. The communities that exist now will move on and change and develop. Their profiles will always continue to alter. Gentrification and social mobility are determinants in the same way as social dependence.

But that deeply embedded culture of being the 'start' of a social journey will remain at the heart of the place, always making it an exciting, gritty and charged area to live in.

Culture of the people needs to be understood and accepted. Peckham is made up of diversity - ethnic, religious, gender, age. Thousands of people pour into Peckham every week, drawn by a retail trade that specialises in ethnic foods and caters for ethnic tastes. There is no defined 'culture of the community', because the community is homogenous. The culture is the diversity, not the sense of same.

For many parts of the community that exists today, it is the combination of 'a starting point' and the fact that there is no defined, recognised culture that creates the real challenges.

There are places all across the UK which faces exactly the same issue. Whether it is Harmsworth in Birmingham, Mosside in Manchester, Toxteth in Liverpool or Glodwick in Oldham; the solutions to these areas is not in trying to fix the cultural issues that exist at this moment in time, but to develop an infrastructure that creates a culture where roots can be established, and the place is more of a settling point rather than a starting point - a warm welcome at the end of a long journey.

For many of the characters in this story, and a large proportion of individuals that I have personally worked with, they have no roots in their local area. There is no history that binds them to the area, or stability that is visible, which gives them the aspiration to move on.

Timi's passion to do well and then come back to make a difference in Peckham is a familiar conversation, because what young people see is that those who do well, move out, turning their back on the next generation, because the culture of 'a place to belong', never existed for them.

The result is that as groups grow up and form friendships, they create their own culture and establish their own morality which has nothing to do with having respect for the community, or the area. That is why robbing someone, assaulting a person, smashing up a fast food outlet, or destroying a play park becomes easy. It is impersonal, there is no relationship, there is no culture of accountability, because this is not their community, or their place. It is the group that matters, they are the actors, the stars of the play, and Peckham is just the stage that they act on.

This is not exclusive to Peckham. There are places across the length and breadth of Britain, where this generational culture is a defining feature. But in most cases the approach is to address what is current and visible rather than address the fundamental point, which is how we create Peckham and these other areas, as a place to stay - a place to dig some roots.

Peckham also faces another cultural challenge - that of the media. Let's be clear about this, the media has not created the gang violence that has developed where young people like Anton senselessly lose their lives. The media has every right - in fact a responsibility - to report on these issues. But there is a real misunderstanding of the actual impact when the media lens is relentlessly pointed at one place, over long periods of time.

When a person, or a family, suffers loss they grieve. Grieving is an essential part of how they overcome that loss, and allowing time for them to grieve is also part of how they deal with loss.

It is no different for a community. The murder of Damilola Taylor - a young 10 year old black boy, who was still in his first 6 months of a new life in the UK - sent shock waves across the nation. But Peckham has never been allowed to heal because for the last 12 years, every time there is a gang story to be written, or a docu-drama to be filmed of 'what it's like living in the toughest estates in Britain', the media descend on Peckham.

As a result the media create an image which is absorbed across middle England - that Peckham is an abhorrent place full of abhorrent people. Those young people growing up in Peckham either vehemently object to the image, or conversely use the image to their advantage; the advantage of notoriety, fear and intimidation.

There is a culture of change sweeping through young people who live in Peckham. It has become a generational change, expressed by young people from primary school to their early twenties, a dramatic transformation, articulated with passion by those passionate for change. Gang affiliation is no longer a 'lifestyle' choice, as it was expressed a few years ago. Knife, gun and gang crime are viewed as socially unacceptable, in a similar way that taking class A drugs is a 'dumb' choice.

However, what young people despise most of all is the way media culture portrays their area. They recognise that this portrayal is actually affecting their lives, both now and in terms of their future. Their view is that when they apply for a job, or a university, or try to make their own first, important step, the media generated stigma defines them.

Whether it is a reality or not, those who are traversing the gap between adolescence and adulthood believe they are experiencing prejudice because of the place them come from. There are many tales of jobs applied for and no interviews, where young people have applied for the same job and had an interview if they use a different post code for their home address, where the best universities give a luke warm response if you reveal you are from SE15, whereas their friend from SE1 gets a conditional offer.

Yes, the media has a responsibility to report on the stories that affect us, but they have a greater social responsibility to ensure that the culture of the media is not affecting our communities.

Let us turn the spotlight onto another aspect of culture - the culture of politics. The view that Timi, Anton, Darell, KJ, Samuel, Andre and all of the other characters in this book are not interested in politics could not be further from the truth. In fact the political culture is one of the most hotly debated topics when you get into the space of being 'respected' by young people on the front line.

Whilst they might talk less about the political characters that seem to obsess so much of the media, they do talk about the absence of political awareness and the irrelevance of politics to their lives, issues and challenges.

Their perception - and they are very perceptive - is that politics focuses on providing an environment where the wider population can aspire to be 'less like them'.

Political decision making and legislative change is to expose the unacceptability of social dependency; to legislate against the anti-social youths that threaten our society, to create academic excellence for those that can afford it, and establish a bindweed of bureaucratic red tape and process that creates stagnation for those that seek the help of the state to get out, move up and move on.

Conversely, young people (and by young people we mean young people up to the age of 25) talk openly and fluently about their own cultural identity.

That identity is about growing up; the groups that form your friendships, the music that you listen to, the faiths that have influenced you, the media images that have portrayed you, the education that has shaped you, the family that has nurtured you and the politics that has infuriated you.

It is like human genes - young people are all unique, shaped by different influences. But at the heart of that uniqueness are the same basic building blocks of their cultural life, social acceptance and aspiration.

Their cultural identity is defined by life's influences and dominated by the need for social acceptance and aspiration. It is diametrically opposed to the political culture that young people - particularly those between the ages of 15 to 25 - see and experience.

Worst of all, they recognise the greed, the power, the bullying, and the in-fighting that makes up politics; the very same traits that politicians condemn them for.

One of the best examples came from a young man who I had been working with in Peckham for several years. We were talking about his ambitions for a university life and his passion for public service beyond that. His motto was and continues to be;

"If you are not part of the solution, then you are part of the problem."

The MP's expenses scandal had been raging for months, and the hilarity over moats and duck ponds had shifted to incredulity that those elected as our representatives in central government, the very people standing up for the 'person on the street', was using every possible way to financially milk the system. The system, of course, is something that the 'person on the street' sees themselves paying for, whilst at the same time making everyday sacrifices to keep food on the table and shelter over their head.

The conversation turned to how young people were translating this now public, 'illegal economy' of MP expenses, to their own lives and experiences. It was a hot topic in the class rooms, college corridors, youth centres, mixing studios, sitting rooms, in front of the gaming consoles and on the front line. The real sting in the tail they felt was that within the space of a few months the virtuous MPs had agreed to terminate the Educational Maintenance Allowance Grant - a small sum of £30 a week, paid to students aged 16 to19 whose family finances made it impossible to fund the basics for student life - buying much needed books or equipment.

Despite the student protests for this grant to continue, their pleas fell on deaf ears. Once more the starkness of reality hit; that their cultural identity and demands for social acceptance and aspiration was ignored and unvalued.

So when there is a murder, when Anton loses his life, or when the government wants to be re-elected, what young people actually see is the culture of political hypocrisy. The hypocrisy is not aimed at the local MP or the ward councillors who turn up to the community hall on a cold February night - they are at least recognised figures who have some stake in the local area. It is aimed at central government and the mandarins at City Hall, whose sweeping statements, sound bites, quick fire policies and commitments bear no resemblance to the cultural identity of young people on the streets in Peckham, Brixton, Hackney, Edmonton Green and New Cross.

Opportunities exist to bring the issue of cultural identity into politics. There are plenty of ways that our 15 to 25 year olds could be drawn into the halls of Westminster, or as work placements into the homogenous government offices of Whitehall. Except that the same bindweed of red tape combined with 'political risk' strangles any such opportunity. After all, imagine what the newspaper headlines would say if they got hold of the story that a 'Pecknarm Gangsta' was working in the sterile environment of the Ministry of Justice, or the Home Office!

So the circle goes on. The media and politics respond to what is in front of them, ignoring cultural history and cultural identity. When there is a crisis, a death, a protest or a riot on the streets, government searches for the cause, when the cause has been expressed for generations.

"You don't understand our identity!"
"You don't understand where we have come from!"

Culture really matters, but understanding how our communities interpret and stamp their own unique definition of culture matter even more. How the big cultural influences affect what we see on the streets and in the lives of people, in our towns and cities.

Whilst each element of culture affects us, as it affects the characters in these pages, the biggest challenge is making sure that cultural identity is not lost.

Above all cultural identity, recognising what makes it, what shapes and moulds it and using its power positively, is the greatest opportunity to influence generations.

Chapter 8
A message From Marline

I cried out for you Andre. That night they took you away.

Some of the olders came to my door. They beat me and raped me, Andre. They raped me right in front of our little girl. There were five of them and they just beat me and raped me, every one of them. I tried to go numb Andre, so that I couldn't feel them, but they were inside me, hurting me and hurting me, I couldn't make them stop.

Our little girl, they just let her see it all. I cried out for you, but you weren't there.

They said they would come back.

I had to leave Andre, please understand, I love you but I had to leave.

Please don't try and find us. I can't deal with the pain and the fear. For the sake of our little girl please, Andre don't try and find us. If you love me, please respect my wishes.

I'm begging you, please Andre, for the sake of our girl, stay away.

Chapter 9
Darell's Story

It was dark and people were screaming, screaming and shouting so loud that it was making my head burst. He was screaming out. There were these flashes of light and explosions like…..like a gas burner igniting on a hob, only louder. I froze. I don't rightly know why, but I froze. Then the boys rushed me. I don't even think they knew I was there but they just rushed me. I saw these glinting lights and the next thing I felt this red hot pain in my thigh and arm and I couldn't stand.

Somehow I got to him. He was crying, just crying and sobbing. He kept on saying,
"Please don't let me die, please don't let me die. I want my mama, please, I don't want to die".

I held him. I don't rightly know if he knew it was me but I held him, told him it would be ok, told him that the ambulance was here. I heard the sirens and some of the flat doors were opened. A lady was screaming and someone tried to help but I wouldn't let him go. I was crying, praying to Jesus not to take his life away. I don't rightly remember when he stopped sobbing. The ambulance came and started doing CPR. I just sat there crying as they took him away.

The paramedic put some strapping around my leg and arm real tight. He put a jacket around me and led me down out of the block. I don't rightly remember anything really. Not right after they took him away. All I remember was feeling numb, like my body didn't belong to me, like I was surrounded in some kind of fog that blanked out everything I could hear, see and feel.

I never saw him again. He died and looking back I wish he had died whilst I was holding him, right there and then, 'cos what they told me, like how he died, cutting him up, I don't rightly know how they could have put him through that.

But I never saw him, I never got a chance to say goodbye. I wanted to say sorry that I'd lied to him, like when I said it would be ok. I knew it wouldn't be ok, I could feel the blood soak into my clothes, warm on my skin and I knew what would happen. I didn't mean to lie to him, but I just didn't know what else I could do, watching his life flow away.

He was my friend you know. I don't just mean my friend like all the others. He was my best friend, my closest friend. He was like my brother - yeah Anton was my brother, my blud. Growing up, there was just me and my mum. We were real close. She treated me like a real adult, none of that shouting at me to do my homework or, not to stay out. I really respected her and she gave me respect.

It wasn't always just the two of us. I had a younger brother Jimi. But he got sickle cell and although they gave him steroids and treatment, his frail little body couldn't cope with it and he died when he was 7. I would have been about 9. It was sad. My mum took it real bad and for a while I was sent back to Nigeria whilst she tried to deal with it.

It was hard you know. I still remember being scared that I was gonna lose my mother and I would be left all alone in the world. I think that's why I took Anton's death real bad. It was like losing Jimi all over.

Yeah, Anton was my brother; he was the one person who made up for Jimi. I shared all my thoughts with him, told him everything, talked about our futures, the clothes we would wear, even had the same style of trainers. I'll never be as close to anyone like I was with Anton.

You know that numbness stayed with me for long time. People came and talked to me and told me what was happening, but I don't rightly know what they were saying. This guy from the council came and talked to me. I asked him why I just felt numb. He said it was the body's way of dealing with the emotional shock, like when you cut yourself the body doesn't feel the pain straight away, because it has a way of protecting itself. He said it's the same with shock, the body has a way of protecting you and that over time the pain will start coming out.

He was right you know. After Anton's funeral, I started to get flash backs. I got angry, real angry with everyone and everything. I got angry with all those people who said Anton and I was their friends, setting us up like that. I got angry with myself because I didn't do more to save him, to put myself on the line for him. I even got angry with my mum for being kind.

I couldn't sleep because I saw these flashbacks, the shots the sounds and the screaming. It's the screaming, I can't get rid of the screaming - it's right here, right here in my head. I started smashing things up. Put my hand through a window, smashed up my things, plates, glasses, anything. Mum would cry and hold me and try and calm me, but the anger wasn't with her, it was with me and all those people who used to be around me.

Then I started crying. It was months later but I started crying. I still had photos of me and Anton on my mobile which I looked at and tried to remember the things we'd done, you know the things we said we would do, places we would go. I wanted to live Anton's legacy, but in my head, when I closed my eyes, all I heard was the screaming.

Yeah, they moved us, me and my mum. Moved us right out to some place in Essex. Mum had a cousin out there who tried to help me. I trust him you know, he's ok, but back then I didn't trust no-one. If I went out walking in the streets, everyone that I saw I thought they were going to shoot me or stab me. If I heard someone shouting or calling out, it totally freaked me out. One time I saw some boys running and I thought they were after me, so I ran for my life, ran into a butcher's screaming for my life. The police came and got me and took me home. I stopped going out after that.

The police were okay. They came and talked to me; took statements. I told them about Anton and our friends. They asked about Samuel and KJ and Timi, Michael and some others who I've never heard of. They never asked about the one person who shot Anton and I never said nothing. I suppose I didn't tell them anything they already knew 'cos they stopped coming. Everyone stopped coming.

I had a counsellor for a while, but they didn't really understand what I was going through. I asked if they had ever been through what I was going through. I just wanted to talk to someone who understood what it was really like, someone who had to deal with the same emotions; tell me what to expect. I wanted to know when I would be able to sleep again, when I could laugh and not feel guilty, when I would stop getting flash backs. But most of all I wanted to know when the screaming would stop.

You know like, looking back when I was growing up around the crew, I think I was surviving. I kept close with them all because it was like, my life depended on it. I didn't do any of the madness that KJ and Samuel and Timi did, but I knew that survival depended on me keeping them close. Do you get me? Samuel had protection through the street rep of his big brother; KJ was protected by Samuel because he was Samuel's front man; Timi had the protection of the olders; even Michael, who had his stuff to deal with, was protected by his music. His music was a talent that Timi and the others exploited; used it to get at other crews to promote their status.

Me, I didn't have any reputation, I didn't have any protection. There weren't any olders I could go running to. I didn't have a talent that gave me respect or an older brother that could beat respect. You know why I joined them? You really know? I joined them because every day that I walked home from my school they would slap me, beat me, steal my stuff, even stole my shoes one time. I never told anyone, never told mum. I was ten, that's all, just ten. I hadn't been back long from being sent away and I was frightened that if I told mum she would send me away again, that she would stop loving me. I was frightened that I would lose the protection of the love of my mum, the only person I had in the world.

So one day when they stopped me I said, "Why are you doing this to me?", and they said, "Because you're not with us." So I became one of them. It wasn't an easy choice - it was the only choice.

I had to do an initiation. Take a mobile phone from someone. I was real scared, but I was more scared of them so I did it. I did a lot of things to stay close to them, but I never beat someone. I stayed close but I never got real close.

Yeah, I carried; just a knife. One from the kitchen; nothing heavy. I had to, not because I was frightened of other groups or anything like that. I carried because I was scared of my own friends. To start with it was KJ who scared me just because of the way he looked at me. His eyes were brown in colour, but when you looked at them you saw they were black inside; real intense black. I thought the black was hate and I feared it. But once I got to know him I realised that it was black with pain, like he was trying to shut off his emotions.

Since Anton died I recognise the same blackness in me. I try and shut the pain away inside me; lock it up. The psychiatrist said I shouldn't, but when I hear the voices and see the faces of those that killed him, I start to panic because I know they will come for me. Yeah, KJ had spent years holding in his emotions and I now realise the truth - that he was too frightened to let them go.

No, I wasn't frightened of KJ, but I was real scared of Samuel. Samuel was off the rails, particularly at the end. He knew he had a reputation and he wasn't going to lose it at any cost. It wasn't always that way. When we were younger I got real close to Samuel, but after we all started going to secondary school it changed. He went to St Michael's and I went to Sacred Heart. The schools were close to each other, but that created a rivalry that split us. Then there was his brother. The word was that he had taken someone's life, so had to flee the country. So Samuel had a street rep and he lived up to its heights.

I was sure one day Samuel would shank me. I was convinced of it. I tried to stay close to him, keep onside, but I was certain that he saw right through me. Saw I was just frightened of him. I held stashes for him. He told me never to look at them and I never did. I used to think that he could see everything that I did; was even watching me when I slept. I would have nightmares about Samuel chasing me, coming after me, getting closer and closer as I kept falling over. I was relieved when he and KJ started travelling, because I got to see less of him.

Samuel had the power. He was evil. He was surrounded by demons. Black Demons.

I knew there would be big trouble after that party around Christmas. Anton had brought his girl with him. I wasn't fond of her. Suppose I was jealous if I'm straight up. Anton and I were still close, but I knew she meant a lot to him and I was frightened I might lose my only real friend. She was okay really, had her own issues, you know what I mean, but she was ok. I think she really liked Anton but tried to hold back, like she wanted him to go after her, wanted him to prove he really wanted her. You understand what I'm saying?

The party was good, real relaxed. We were all chilling, talking through stuff - life, music, the stupidness of the police and government - you know the usual stuff. We never talked about ourselves, about how we felt, the really important things. We never talked about our demons. Anton and his girl were real close, but it was like he was bringing her in, rather than she was taking him out. Everything was good, we were drinking and smoking. We all smoked, you know like weed and stuff. We never did heavy drugs, like, that was for the street junkies, not for us.

Yeah, the party was going real good, Michael even took the mic and performed some of his stuff. Everyone was whooping and hollering. He was the best and back in the day, no one could touch him.

When Samuel came in the whole mood changed. One look at him and you knew he had come for trouble. I could see all of his dark spirits around him, their blackness and evil swooping around. I know others could see them and I could see the life of others shrinking back inside them retreating from Samuel and his demons, like they were hiding away, frightened of his power.

You probably think I'm not right don't you, me talking about spirits like this? But you gotta understand that they are real, just as real and just as alive as you and me. See dark spirits come from the soul, right inside you. You can deal with your dark spirits through positive spirits; things you do every day that are good. You build an army of positive spirits and they are what makes you know right from wrong, because every dark spirit needs a hundred good spirits to fight it down. But when you let the dark spirits take over they turn your soul black. They choke your heart. They turn every thought into hate and revenge and envy and greed.

You think this sounds like some African voodoo madness? But I can see the spirits and I've seen exorcisms. There are special people that are trained to exorcise the spirits, do rituals, give you rings and charms. Some of them are from the churches and some are elders who have inherited the power. They remove the spirits by prayer and chants and laying hands. I've seen it; I've seen a woman surrounded by demons, watched them being dragged screaming from her. I've seen a man shaking and screaming as a pastor ripped the dark spirits from inside him, cursing and wailing. Some of the priests banish them, others absorb them inside themselves, knowing that they have enough good spirits to fight them and kill them.

Samuel went to a reader. It was after Anton's murder. He started wearing a ring to protect him. It was a tribal ring and he talked about how it would see him through the court trial. He even had a pastor attend court to extract the information and make potions to protect him. He gave the family sections of the bible that would have the greatest influence and bring spirits to influence the court.

If I could have taken Samuel and had his spirits exorcised before, perhaps I could have saved Anton. But I didn't, I was too frightened of him, knowing my spirits weren't strong enough and they would leave me, run away and stop trying to help me. Samuel stood in that party spreading fear and hate, but no one did anything, no one had the rep to move him on.

I heard people saying that Samuel and Anton had a bust up over his girl. Timi said it but you need to know that it wasn't true. Timi had ulterior motives and wanted Anton's girl for himself. But she didn't want him so he spread these lies. No, you know why Samuel kicked off with Anton? Well truth is Samuel accused Anton of drinking from his can; said they were on the same table and Anton drank from his can. Man he kicked off big time and no matter what everyone said to keep it loose he just tore it up. Samuel faced up to Anton and I could see any moment he was either going to shank him or glass him. Me and Michael pulled Anton out, dragged him out of the party whilst Samuel was cussing him calling him a pussy, saying he was calling Anton's name, that he was marked. I saw Timi standing next to Samuel. Timi's soul was hidden by Samuels power, like he no longer existed.

Despite there being a truce, I knew it was the end. We were all just waiting time, you know? I had dreams of what would happen, but in my dreams I was the one with the blood flowing out of me, staining the pavement and soaking my clothes. I saw myself lying and pleading for my mum. But it wasn't me, it was Anton, and if I could have the time again I would have taken the bullet for him. It would have been better than being locked in this nightmare and the constant screaming in my head.

After I slashed my wrists, I got taken into this place. I'd been here a few months when they let me back home. They had moved mum and it was like a new start in a safe place. It was great at first, but then I started seeing these people watching me and following me; seeing things that scared me; like people were after me. Once I thought Anton was coming after me, trying to pull me down into his grave. Sometimes I think Anton is still alive and following me, tracking my every move. Sometimes I am convinced that I can see him out of the corner of my eye. Things would have been real different if Anton was still alive.

I stole a car and crashed it. I don't know why I stole it, but I think I saw it as an escape. Things got bad, and the demons started taking over me again. It was after I beat my mum I came back here. It's not like a hospital or anything and the people here are trying to help me. They wouldn't let me see my mum to start with as they said I need a time of 'orientation'. I like that word.......'orientation'. I know what they mean; I need to find a way of ordering things in my head so that I can move on.

Man, I don't know how I am supposed to deal with all this loss. Every page of my life there is loss. I don't understand why I have to bear all of this! Why has God laid this on me? I'm not ready to deal with all of this right now. Every day it feels like it raining. I can look outside of the window, at that frightening world outside and I see rain falling. You can tell me the sun is shining but all I see is the dark sky and rain relentlessly falling. Some days, on good days, it's just fine drizzle - enough to let the light through. But on bad days the rain is torrential, like a monsoon, flooding my head, filling my world with blackness and I can't see any way out. I hear people in my head, telling me that I need to escape, find an escape, a way out, to get away of all of this pain and hurt and darkness. I have tried ways to escape. But people stop me and the hurt just comes back even stronger.

I know Samuel and KJ are in prison now. I don't really feel anything for them because they killed my best friend. They turned my world into a nightmare with all of their evil and hate. But I don't understand how the person who actually pulled the trigger, the person who took Anton's life can live with himself. How can you be that close to someone and take his life?

Do you think he hears the screaming inside his head like some perpetual nightmare? I don't rightly know how he can walk the streets, knowing he took Anton's life, even if he never meant it to happen. I hope it haunts him forever like it haunts me; the darkness that is choking me, pressing down on me so I can't breathe and all I can hear is the screaming, the constant screaming. I hope he hears it, inside him like I do, locked up inside him, never able to get out. The only time it will be released will be the day that he dies.

Chapter 10
Emotional Rescue

Working with Darell has been one of the greatest and most challenging of journeys. His story is not an isolated one. In fact, the reality is there are hundreds of Darells who suffer the loss of a friend or family member to gang violence.

The hard part of working with Darell is that encapsulated in the life of this one young person is the emotional fragility that exists in us all. That fragility is ultimately defined by the tragedies that we face, and the resilience of our closest family and friends that help us overcome them.

Darell's ability to manage the pressure cooker of life that he faced, growing up in a fractured community in south London, was through making choices that he knew - from the time that he made them - were actually not his personal choices at all. He recognised that the decisions to befriend a gang, to carry a knife, to courier drugs and stay close to certain key individuals were all taken as a form of acquiescence; a submission of his morality and will in order to survive.

These decisions on their own were not enough to create the emotional fragility that existed for him. That fragility had been created long before, when his brother died and, in his eyes, his mother abandoned him. Darell was carrying deep seated emotional trauma from the age of 9 but like many of the young adults who become ensconced in gang violence, this trauma went unrecognised. In fact, those that identified it the most, exploited it. They saw it as a weakness that they could use to get Darell to carry weapons, courier drugs and act as a cover for their own criminality.

Darell's story is not an isolated one, because emotional trauma, the third of our 5 dynamic factors, is written in large bold letters in the life histories of so many of the individuals and families involved in violent street gangs. Loss is one of the crucial denominators. Loss of a family member, or of a close friend, can evoke the strongest emotional energy which, if not focused in the right direction can develop into a deep seated resentment and bitterness. Loss and bereavement creates an intensity of pain, as acute as any physical injury, and like a physical injury, it needs to be healed. If not, the emotional wound becomes infected - gangrenous - eating away at the person unchecked and leading to a distorted view of the world and the people in it.

The fact is our approach to bereavement and loss, particularly for adolescents and young adults, is archaic. We take this issue and envelope it into the world of counselling or psychiatric assessment. Alternatively we proffer advice on 'wrap around' support from family members or through schools, those who we profess have an established bond and relationship. When the individual does not fit into the assessment criteria of the former, the professionals turn to the latter, often placing the responsibility at the door of those who are the least emotionally equipped to deal with it.

Darell's mother could offer no support to him, because her grief was so intense that she lost all perspective on the needs of her son. Her loss created an emotional numbness which took her years to deal with. As a result, Darell had to find solace elsewhere; a task made infinitely worse by the fact that he faced the added loss of his mother, whose disappearance from his life for over 6 months, felt like abandonment. Inside, he felt that the reason his mother had left him was that he was to blame for his brother's death; a feeling of guilt that he carried with him and only came to the fore in his psychiatric sessions a decade later.

As a young child and adolescent, Darell was never assessed for counselling or professional support. Even if he had been, the chances are that he would not have achieved the threshold for such support; a threshold which has been set by professionals based on statutory guidelines, with little understanding of the pressures that young adults like Darell, and so many like him, have to face as they grow up.

The stark reality is that Darell is far from an isolated case. There are thousands of young people and young adults who have had to face loss and bereavement with little support, and, in the vast majority of cases, little recognition, of the long term emotional damage that it can have on them. Whilst for some celebrating a person's life can be a focus, there are an equal number who feel that revenge is the only true form of justice and the only tangible way in achieving personal absolution. After all, the person was their "blud", their "bro", part of their "fam" - his death needed to be avenged. God says, "an eye for an eye".

Providing the emotional support that is required - delivered by people who have a genuine understanding and empathy of the loss faced by these young people - still seems to be beyond the grasp of government, and the agencies tasked with the responsibility of preventing the manifestation of street violence. As a result we perpetuate the problem, because we know the vacuum exists. Instead of filling it with the support that is needed, we surround it with existing services and processes, assessments and case conferences and 'wrap around interventions'. All of these are designed to absolve the myriad of agencies of their responsibilities, through discussions on "ineligibility" and not "reaching the threshold", review periods and monitoring.

Bereavement and loss are not the only factors that create emotional trauma. Sadly, abuse and domestic abuse are an even greater constant in early childhood for many of the real life characters who go on to inflict violence. The truth is that, in around 75% of the cases, the young person has witnessed domestic abuse, seen their mother, brother or sister beaten, or suffered themselves at the hands of an abuser. The abuse is not just a one off, but part of the fabric of their childhood and early years, to such an extent that they become highly sensitised to the emotionally charged atmosphere and pressure that comes with the violence - but desensitised to the violence itself.

As a consequence their demeanour is of someone who is always on edge; a tightly coiled spring, swift to respond to the slightest provocation through highly tuned reflexes, with the ability to inflict pain without feeling any remorse. Unchecked, the abused becomes the abuser, because life has taught them that violence is the only way to deal with conflict, and through generations, the cycle is perpetuated.

This cycle is not exclusive to young men who become involved in gang violence. Gang violence is not gender specific. Some young women who experience the same emotional journey, reinterpret being hit as a sign of affection; of love. After all, as one young women explained to me:

"...he hits me 'cos he's jealous dat I might love someone else".

The reality, however, is that for those who have grown up in violent households, both sexes are subjected to a level of trauma which can only be avoided by using basic human instincts - the instincts of survival. As a result, they do not have the experiences of the subtleties of love, affection, mutual respect, trust and responsibility that come from stable relationships, because they have never experienced a stable relationship. The long term impact is that their own future relationships are built on the misconception that conflict and violence, coercion and control are a predeterminate of a healthy relationship. And so the cycle continues.

Young women are just as susceptible to the draws of gang involvement - the excitement of being nonconformist and challenging authority and gender stereotypes.   The sense of belonging; of being recognised; having a stake and a voice, is just as strong in young women as young men. For some, just the association is enough, after which they can move on. For others, becoming pregnant and having a child, who then becomes wholly reliant on them, is a cathartic experience. It creates a maternal bond that changes the emotional dependence, providing them with a status in society - a mother - responsible and demanding respect.

Despite all of the violence and brutality that surrounds gang lifestyle, it is a sobering thought that having a child is still one of the biggest catalysts for change, for coming "off road". That emotional connection provides one more opportunity to prove that you can protect someone you love; to put right the deep seated feeling of impotency that has been held in check over the years - from experiencing violence in your home, the death of a close friend, or seeing you mother, brother or sister suffer through chronic ill health. Although the willingness to provide support is in abundance, neither the young woman nor the young man has the experience of what it takes to be an emotional and financial provider. They do not have the emotional capital that is built over a generation of stability, through a strong, cohesive, family environment. Their best intentions become challenged by their personal frustrations, which they exorcise in the only way that they have learnt - through confrontation, intimidation and violence. And so the cycle continues.

Much has been written about the sexual exploitation of young women through gangs, but little is articulated around the emotional and psychological journey that results in young women making choices to become involved with high risk young men, entering into subsequently high risk relationships. Perhaps it is the fact that for some it is a choice that they willingly make, just like it is a choice for some young men, that makes it all the more uncomfortable for us to talk about.

So, if a stable family environment is so important, are we not missing a vital voice in this story - the voice of the father? There are so few father figures shown in the lives of Darell, KJ and his sisters, Timi, Anton and Michael because the harsh reality is that their fathers are absent, without exception. They have abstained themselves from their responsibility, and in some cases - like KJ's father - they have granted themselves personal absolution from guilt. They cite a range of excuses for their distance, such as, by staying, they would have created a hostile home environment, or they had no job, no money, and the financial pressures of bringing up a family were too great. They rarely discuss the emotional damage of their absence, in part because they themselves do not have the emotional capacity to deal with it. But it is also because admitting that they have neglected their responsibility would be to expose a shame on themselves, which they know is personally reprehensible.

Family breakdown, or the lack of a stable male role model, has become the norm. Alongside it we see the likes of KJ, Andre, Timi, Anton and Samuel trying to fulfill the stereotypical male role - the bread winner, the man of the household, the responsible adult. They are placed in this position at the most tender of ages - 8, 9, 10,11 or sometimes even younger - when they are neither emotionally equipped or bestowed with the knowledge of how to fulfil this role. As a result, their inability to provide support and protection turns to feelings of personal inadequacy, frustration, failure and quite often violent behaviour, which all reinforce the fact that they were and remain emotionally ill-equipped to handle such responsibility.

This is compounded upon, as each of these young people also struggles to address the fundamental breakdown that the loss of their father has caused to their mother and siblings. None of them receives emotional support, in the same way that there is no emotional support for those suffering bereavement. So they console themselves on the streets, surrounded by kindred spirits who bear the same loss and the same inadequacies. They do not need to share their feelings, but they can combine their frustrations, anger and bitterness, corralling their negative energy to commit unprovoked acts of violence for the most innocuous things; a glance that is construed as disrespect; the wrong conversation with another's girlfriend; or drinking from the wrong can.

They may use violence in the most brutally remorseless ways, but what life has taught them is a self-loathing, because they see the continuous breakdown in the relationships around them as their fault. They see themselves as the cause, because they were incapable of making things better, because they had not reached an age of maturity that enabled them to protect, provide or support.

They cannot love others because through their emotional experience they do not love themselves, and so, unchecked, their inadequacy is compounded through the relationships that they form. These relationships are based on mistrust and suspicion - emotions that relate to how they feel about themselves - and which act as a barrier to those who might want to get close to them. Timi, Darell, Anton, KJ, Samuel and Michael stayed close for all of the years of their adolescence. They were friends, but they also knew each other's capabilities and the consequences of trying to find their own path, separate from that tightly entwined peer group. The fear and suspicion that that they held towards each other was as great a hold as the loyalty and respect that they outwardly projected.

Andre's girlfriend, Marline, wanted a relationship with him. She saw good in him from early on, but she knew that she had to wait until his vulnerabilities were exposed; just enough to allow his real emotional being to shine through.

Andre, KJ, Darell, Timi and Samuel were not born bad. Their exposure to poly-traumatic experiences from an early age - such as loss, neglect, bereavement, violence, abuse, emotional detachment, and family breakdown - taught them to chain and lock tightly inside their softer, more vulnerable emotions. In their place they used what life had taught them - fight for everything; trust no one; respect nothing; get what you need at any cost.

Andre and his brother Kelvin were exposed to some of the harshest of emotional experiences. They saw their father butchered in front of their eyes, sliced up like a piece of meat. They had to learn to survive, in a household where their mother was a crack addict and a prostitute. They were forced to leave their grandparents behind; the only people who showed them truly unlimited love and affection. Instead they came to a foreign world, where they were exposed to even greater risks, living in a crack den surrounded by violence and crime.

The fact that they survived at all is a testimony to their own personal resolve and reliance on each other. They became good at concealing the daily degradation that they were subjected to, not because of a fear of the involvement of services, but because of the personal humiliation that they would suffer. They chose to build an emotional brick wall around themselves, to protect the life that they lived, and it was only at the times when their vulnerability was beginning to be exposed, that they then hit out, using violence and criminality as a shield.

For KJ, his daily battle was the ill health of his mother and the impact that had on him and his sisters' approach to life, and more profoundly, death. His mother's suffering, and the fact that her illness was both degenerative and terminal, resulted in KJ's personal feelings of impotency and powerlessness. Whilst his sisters took on the nurturing role for their mother and the family, KJ was left to adopt the male role model; the provider, the protector. His own suffering, as he slowly watched his mother deteriorate, was never discussed. His closest sister put up her own emotional protection, focused on practicalities, jobs to be done, meals to be cooked, money to be earned. KJ had no male role model to turn to. Once as a small child, he had respect for his father, but that changed, irrevocably, replaced by humiliation when he saw him in the street, supermarket, or takeaway shop. Every sighting left him feeling ashamed.

Like the life histories of the other characters, KJ's is far from unfamiliar. Ill health in families is becoming a common feature in the backgrounds of young adolescents involved in gang violence, both male and female. In the past, the focus has been on mental ill health, but more recently the impact of cannabis in terms of psychosis has come to the fore.

Sadly, chronic ill health, cancer, sickle cell, lupus, Parkinson's and a myriad of other degenerative illnesses are equally as common. For many adolescents the daily pressure of living with chronic ill health, often in a single parent household is an immense emotional drain, which requires empathetic support and guidance, but which are rarely offered or provided.

There is a daily reminder of just how powerless they are, despite their willingness to take away the suffering. That powerlessness is replaced by a sense of worthlessness that nags at them to the point where being at home is emotionally suffocating; only bearable by finding ways to dull the pain. Skunk becomes a useful ally, until it becomes a daily norm. Sleeping over at friends becomes weekends away, then weeks of sofa surfing. Couriering drugs out of London lifts the oppression; the consequences of being caught are no greater than returning home to face the grim reality of the inevitable. Ultimately, the heartbreak of watching a loved one suffering is too much to bear.

For some, like Samuel and Andre, they not only had to rationalise their experiences of violence from an early age, they also had to cope with the emotional trauma of leaving their homes and travelling to a new country, and a new way of life. As young children they did not have the stability of a familiar home life - attending a familiar school, growing up on streets whose familiarity provides a sense of safety. You will read the stories of two young boys and their brothers who saw the brutality of the world and who then had to cope with being taken across continents, to an environment which was alien and incomprehensible. The only weapon that they had at their disposal with which to hammer out their own personal identity in this new hostile world was the one they had learnt - the weapon of violence. So for the next few years they developed their familiarity with violence. They felt a sense of safety and belonging by using violence and intimidation, gaining an air of indomitability that helped conceal their emotional immaturity. Even at the times when they wanted to move on, they did not have the experience of a stable home life or stable relationships to draw on. Instead, their frustration turned to anger and their anger turned to violence. And so the cycle continues.

A review of case histories will tell you that in virtually every incident where there has been a tragic death related to urban gang violence, poly-emotional trauma features in the backgrounds of either the victim or the accused, or sadly, in both.

Providing emotional support is well within our capability. There is an abundance of people who have experienced similar loss, and with the right support could console and provide empathy. There is an array of counsellors who have life experiences to guide young people, and their families and younger siblings, through loss. Our failure to harness this creates the worst of vacuums - a tragic place where some of those friends and siblings become filled with revenge, hatred and embitterment, distrust and a lack of remorse; traits that will ultimately lead to more violence, more tragedy and more loss of life.

For some, the solace of a family member or a school counsellor is valued, but for others they need personal one to one support, by people who can give time and have empathy.

The truth is that we all have the gift to provide some form of emotional rescue. Humanity is ultimately based on the principle of our ability to empathise, to offer some compassion and human kindness. One close friend who has worked in this field for many years once said:

"A person should not be judged by how much they see of the world. They should be judged by how much they see of the world through the eyes of others."

Unlike all of the other causes of gang violence, emotional support is the only one where we all have the personal ability to make a difference. It does not require government to lead, or provide 'sustainable' funding streams, set up working groups, or invest in multi-million pound research programmes, to tell us what we already know. It does not need the public sector to step in and provide 'wrap around' support and then be ostracised for intervening in the first place.

Reflecting on the painful journeys that these young adolescents have faced, what they themselves collectively and unanimously say, is that if they just had someone who had compassion, who cared and who could have given them some time, it would have made a life changing difference; a life-saving difference.

Can something that simple be so beyond us?

Chapter 11
A Police Officer's Story

Do I think he was guilty?

Yes, he was guilty; personally I'm convinced of it.

The whole team was. But there is a big difference between knowing that someone has been involved in a murder and proving it. The public might feel frustrated by that, but it's a fact. There are plenty of people out there who know who pulled the trigger that night and if they really wanted to make a difference they should get in touch with us, so we can take another dangerous criminal off the streets. That's why we are here, to take bad people off the streets to stop other people getting hurt.

I joined the police in 1993. I grew up in Edmonton, not far from Lea Valley. My dad was a big influence in my life. He was a grafter, a builder by trade who worked hard every day of his life. He liked a pint and had a local pub, 'The Ferryman', which he went to on Friday nights and every Sunday lunchtime before the family meal.

My grandmother lived down Seven Sisters Road in the same house she was born in. She was 100 when she died in 1997. She has lived out two world wars and 4 monarchs, two husbands and everyone in the family of her generation. She was as tough as old boots, but with a heart of gold. She loved all of her grandchildren, but I know she had a real soft spot for me.

I still remember the family gatherings and parties at Christmas. As I got older I would go and spend the weekend at her house. In the summer, she would take me, my brother and our cousin down to the coast. We would go to Brighton, Eastbourne or Southend, getting on the tube at Manor House at the crack of dawn and then the train from Victoria. Broadstairs was her favourite; a wide sandy beach and a fish and chip shop to die for.

She had this old shopping trolley on wheels that she would pack up with sandwiches and drinks, chocolate, towels, spades, buckets and God knows what else. We would spend all day at the coast and then head back at about 6, arriving home at 8 when she would make a huge batch of pancakes for us, sending us to bed with the warmth of the sun still on our faces and full and contented stomachs, ready to start again on another adventure the next day.

If we didn't go to the coast we would visits the museums or the art galleries, wander through Covent Garden, Portobello Market or Brick Lane on a Sunday. We would spend the whole summer living out of her house on Berkeley Road. It was a dirty shabby little house, full of mice, an old stove with a grill propped up with a tin can and a TV on so loud that you could hear it in the street. But it was the best place in the world to me; full of warmth and adventure.

Gran would tell us her stories about the bombings in the Blitz; how she signed up to be a nurse and would walk the three miles there and back to the Middlesex Hospital with a tin basin on her head stuffed with cotton wool. She would tell us about her first husband who owned his own hackney carriage in 1918 - a horse and cart stabled in Stoke Newington. She told us stories of local people, her fights with the council and Bernie Grant, like they were yesterday. She taught us pride in our history and sticking up for what was right.

I suppose all of those trips and visits ingrained in me a sense of being a Londoner; a proud Londoner. It's the smells and the taste of London that I sense all around me, not just the sights and the landmarks. Every area of London has a uniqueness and in my career I've had the privilege of working in lots of different areas, from Waltham Forest to Lambeth, Southwark and Hackney. I've worked in specialist units like SCD7, chasing the bad guys who supply drug markets, to SCD8, Trident, running a team tackling black on black shootings.

Look, I know it's not PC to say these things, but the fact is my family ground into me the values of respect and morals of right and wrong. They taught me to appreciate the things around me, our neighbours and what it meant to have family values. Don't get me wrong, if either my brother or I would step out of line, we were for it. Mum had three different spatulas that she would use to beat us, depending on how much trouble we were in - a wooden one, plastic one, or a metal one. It was mum that chastised us. On the whole dad left her to it. But if we ever disrespected mum, then he wouldn't take any prisoners. But the worst of all was from Gran; a tongue lashing that outstripped any physical beating from our parents.

A lot of these kids nowadays don't have respect. A lot of them don't come from here. Their families come across from Africa or India or Pakistan. They have a different attitude to life and the police. A lot of them don't have their dad and their families are still back home. So they don't get taught respect like it was when I grew up. They should teach something useful when these families come over, like how to parent properly and how to respect authorities.

Morals and respect were a big part of my upbringing. I know that these were part of my decision to join the police. I wanted a career that would give me progression, but also one that earned respect. I was at school in Edmonton in October 1985 when the Broadwater Riots broke out. I remember the sense of excitement amongst my friends when we talked about it. My gran's attitude was very different. She was all for people arguing for their rights and peaceful protests, but killing a policeman who was just trying to protect his local community was just not on.

Those riots had a big influence on me, like there was a whole different world going on right in my back yard, which I knew nothing about. Looking back, that was the time when I started to think that the police force was the kind of career for me. I didn't talk about it with my mum, but my dad and I discussed it. He said that protecting and preserving life was a respectable profession, but he also warned me that those that are involved in dealing with criminals are also susceptible to criminals, and if I wanted to stick to my principles I would have to be wary of what I was getting involved in. He couldn't have been more right.

I left college at 21, with a HND in Estate Management. It was nothing special, but I suppose I had always known that college was a bit of light relief before my real career. I applied for the police in the summer of 1992 and eventually went off to Hendon Training College in 1993. I spent the autumn getting myself fit, studying some law and partying hard. By the time I started as a new recruit in March of '93, I was ready, mentally and physically. The initial training was for 12 weeks. It was okay, not as tough as I thought, but there was so much law to learn. That was the hard part.

After training I spent two years as a probationer in Hackney working out of Stoke Newington police station. I worked the reactive teams, doing ten hour shifts, chasing calls across the borough, from fights in pubs to domestics, burglaries to snatches. We chased down the bad guys, or talked the drunken clubbers from kicking the shit out of each other. It was tough, but after two years I had seen every walk of life. I was a good looking fresh faced PC and got propositioned by prostitutes and lonely housewives in equal measure.

By the time my probation period was up I had already got a reputation for sniffing out drugs. If there was a stash in a house, or on a person, or in a car, I would always be the one to find it. I got the nickname 'Sniffer Hughes'. I had already decided that I wanted to be become a detective, but as far as my bosses were concerned, I hadn't done my time yet. I spent another 18 months as a PC as part of a sector team, working on a patch around Clapton - an area notoriously known as 'murder mile'.

By then it was 1996/7, the year after the Brixton riots. It was the first time that I had been involved in policing a full blown riot. I was on duty that day in September and remember sitting in a carrier being driven down the Brixton Road from the Oval to what looked like a war zone. This black guy called Wayne Douglas had collapsed and died at Brixton Police Station, where he was being questioned about a burglary. There was a march down Brixton Road to the police station, after which the violence started with black youths shouting "killers" at us. We were assigned to part of a cordon along Acre Lane that sealed off the area all around Brixton town centre.

There were missiles being thrown and - as I learnt later - one part of the cordon on Brixton Road had petrol bombs thrown at them. We heard shots being fired. I was scared shitless. What hit me was the hate that was on all of those black faces that were confronting us. It was a sea of black faces, some with masks or scarves or bandanas, but I could still see their eyes and the hatred they had for the police.

I know the police aren't perfect, I'm not saying we haven't got things wrong over the years, sometimes we've got them really wrong, you can't deny it. Some members of the community still think we are prejudiced, despite all of the lessons learnt from the Tottenham and Brixton Riots and the Lawrence inquiry. But you have to understand the facts. If you look at the daily crime reports like I do, or the photo fits of our robbers and gang nominals, the vast majority are black IC3 males. You look at other crime types its different. For example, theft other, the suspects are white, 19-29 year olds, alcohol violence related to the night time economy, its white males 18-34, although I have to say we are seeing more young women nowadays.

83% of our robberies in Lambeth are carried out by suspects described as IC3 males in their late teens to early twenties. That's a fact. So when our boys and girls are out, following leads on following leads on robbery suspects and gang suspects, the will target those that match the description of the suspects. If we get a description of a knife point robbery from a victim who says those that threatened him, or her, were a group of IC3 males in their late teens we are hardly going to stop a group of white lads are we? If a victim were to describe his or her attackers as a group of IC1's, then we are going to go after a group of white lads who match the description.

I know there are people out there who think this is discrimination. But it isn't. Listen, you go to other parts of the country you will find gang nominals who are white, you go to somewhere else they will be Asian. Back in the 1930's there were Jewish, Irish and Italian gangs, running racecourse betting scams. There was even a girl gang from Walworth called the Forty Elephants. What we are dealing with now is just a point in time. Chances are, in 10 years' time, the profile will be different.

As investigators we have to work on the facts that we are presented with. It's not rocket science that we are going to go after the people who match the description. That's the fact; end of.

Truth is many of the victims of gang violence are of the same ethnic background as the suspects. In fact, there is a disproportionate number of IC3 victims. In recent years, most of the cases we deal with are internal gang feuds. So we have a pretty good idea that the suspects will be a similar description, if not already well known to us. Our source intelligence gives us a good head's up in most cases. The hard part is getting the right evidence that we can will convince the CPS that its in the public interest to prosecute.

I'd spent about 10 years working as a Detective Constable, Sergeant and then Inspector in borough based C.I.D's. My old boss got a post in SCD7 and after I passed my Chief Inspector exams, he tapped me up to come and join him. By this time I was married and living in Seven Kings. I had two kids, 6 and 4. My wife was pretty understanding when we first met, but when the kids came along she had to pack up her job. What with me working 16 hour shifts and long weekends, we inevitably developed separate lives. I knew things weren't going well between us, but the job makes it all the harder to really change. It's not like I can work from home or take a weekend off. We're not like some council workers, sitting at home one day a week pretending to write a report, when they are off down the pub or minding the kids.

I tried to keep holidays and Christmas's clear, but if a critical incident happened it was my head on the line. It's always been that way in the Met. It's relentless. It's the middle ranked officers that do all of the really hard graft. If we get it right the superiors get the pats on the back, and if we get it wrong we get named and shamed. Look at the Sapphire Unit in Southwark; the bosses made the decision on clear up rates for rape cases and when things went tits up, it was the DCI who took all the flak. I'm telling you, cutting out middle ranking officers is the worst thing that Boris and his mob could do. He's never been a front line police officer, or a hard working DCI, so what would he know? Life's never been a bed of roses in the Met, but you just have to take the wins when they come along, after all of the hard graft from the boys and girls in the team.

In SCD7, I was put in charge of a team with the task of disrupting the cannabis market. Even in 2007 we could see just how fast the cannabis market was exploding. It's not cannabis like back in the Woodstock days, none of your herbal remedy stuff. This is skunk, hydroponically grown in well-designed environments, where growing it in a two bed flat on the Pembury Estate can turn you a profit of over £800,000 a year. This is big business. It's run by family syndicates who front fund their local organisations to take over properties and run franchises, which can grow and harvest a crop every 8 weeks. With a network of 6-8 houses, they can have a crop worth £100,000 street value, each week, every week. Selling cannabis is a gateway to open up Class A drug lines. May of the nominals we do TP's on operate drug lines across the home counties, to the cost west country; even to Wales. They call it "going country"; couriering drugs to market town where the local police aren't resources are switched on enough to tackle them and where the locals aren't organized enough to resist them.

The organised crime networks around skunk and class A drugs has moved a long way from the grow your own cottage industry or the crack houses of the late 90's. It's a multi-million pound criminal business, with one of the organisations having their own scientists who help mutate the female cannabis plants to maximise their potency. Some of the drug lines are highly sophisticated, holding several addresses, one doing a deal, one holding the cash and one holding the drugs. Each address changes every few days, but the common feature is these addresses are often the homes of very vulnerable people who are intimidated, assaulted and degraded by these low lifes.

Yeah we are definitely feeling the full force of skunk. A lot of the nominals that we target in Trident have a chronic skunk habit and clearly have mental health problems - psychosis, paranoia and schizophrenia.

Taking out drug dealers has become just as important as taking out class A supply chains, because the criminals don't care about who gets hurt as long as the money rolls in. At one time they even started lacing the cannabis with crack, just to get people more hooked and to 'diversify' their business.

I won't hide it, taking these scrum bags of the streets is a real pleasure.

My unit took out whole supply chains that ran across the length and breadth of the UK and beyond, from the street dealers, all the way through to the head of the chain - the one who ran the teams across whole regions not just a small strand on an estate. These guys would have a series of houses spread across an area, never staying in the same place for long and always varying their patterns. They would have numerous mobile phones, different numbers for different supply lines and they would change their numbers every couple of weeks. Sometimes they would get sloppy and we would track them down. It might be they had a car they really liked and stuck with it for too long, or a mobile which they kept for personal stuff but carelessly gave the number away. One idiot stored large batches of cannabis in his lock up on an estate but forgot to pay the council the rent for it. So one day a housing officer opened up the garage and found 5 tonnes of the stuff inside.

But most of the time we tracked them through hard graft, TP's, test purchase operations, 24 hour surveillance teams working for months on end, and using specialists in phone forensics. It was 16 hour days for months on end.

By 2008, my marriage was well and truly over. It was an amicable split, no dramas. I still loved my wife and kids but I knew that the job had driven a chasm between us that we could never fill. I moved into a friend's house for a couple a months - a police colleague, who I was a probationer with all those years ago. That's one good thing about the job; you end up with real friends for life. I moved into a flat in a new development in Canning Town, really easy to look after and enough space for the kids to stay over. That was about four years ago and I still laugh with them that it won't be long before I finally unpack!

I got a good reputation in SCD7. I even got a Commissioner's Commendation for taking out a national supply chain which was being run from a mansion in Surrey, funded by some well-heeled posh boy who was using his annual allowance as the investment. God knows how he never got convicted. Sometimes you can't believe what this business turns over.

When my old boss moved over to SCD8 he arranged it that my whole unit went with him. SCD8 is Trident, dealing with black on black shootings. I arrived in 2009 and the team was in serious meltdown. The previous year there had been the highest number of teenage murders in the capital; the vast majority gang related and Trident were at the sharp end of getting kick over it. A new Trident Commander had just come in - Commander Helen Ball. She wasn't like any of the old commanders that the unit had. She was calm and measured, no drama and she wanted the unit to get its head down and focus on the work, not the hype. My boss had been brought in to grip the unit and tighten up on practices and performance. My team was seen as outsiders and we got the cold shoulder for a few weeks; not something I wasn't expecting. It was the same when I moved to SCD7. But once the more established members of the team recognised our abilities and the fact that we got results, we were soon accepted.

What we did realise was that a lot of the bad guys that we were pursuing in SCD7 were exactly the same as the ones that SCD8 were after. You've got to understand that when you are involved in covert ops, the rule is that you don't share your intel with anyone outside of the team. I've worked on loads of ops where someone has been indiscreet and we've had to pull officers out. You have to keep things tight. Sharing intel is a no-no. I get it that people in the community or the council want to know more, but that just isn't possible and will never happen. You want us to catch the criminals, we need to make sure that we don't leak how we are doing it, end of.

The Bakara case is a typical one. I'd been in SCD8 about 18 months when I got the case. By then I'd been working in the South East proactive team and heading up on the investigation of several murders, mainly in Lambeth if I'm truthful. The cases aren't that different in terms of how we approach them. Forensics is the key and in the early stage, the more we can do to preserve the scene the better. On the Bakara case we had multiple scenes - the stairwell when the shots were fired, the stairs and entrance door where there were traces of blood, and then a fingertip search of the estate to find the weapon.

Frankly, we could have done without Richards walking all over the crime scene to get to Bakara. God knows how much damage was done in lost evidence. Richards was arrested on the spot and taken to King's College Hospital. He had superficial stab wounds, but we couldn't be certain that he wasn't involved in the actual shooting. Our investigators interviewed him at the hospital. We didn't get anything out of him at the time, which is pretty typical to be quite honest. We put a police guard on him just in case some of the crew tried to come for him at the hospital. It's not unheard of, you know, fights breaking out in A&E when a gang turn up and start threatening staff. The boundaries with this lot are pretty limitless.

Anyway, we dismissed Richards pretty early on. The blood on his clothes was his and Bakara's, but we did get some interesting fibres back and his mobile was very helpful, but I'll come to that in a minute.

The crime scene itself gave us some key insights. Bakara was shot at close range, so we knew that the chances were that there would be gunshot residue on the clothes of the suspect, or suspects. Two casings were found on the scene, one of the bullets had passed through Bakara and we recovered one in a door frame; good work from a sharp eyed member of the forensic team. Combined with the post mortem, we knew pretty early on that the person who shot

Bakara was likely to be of a similar height, so Richards was a non-starter because he was four inches shorter.

The casings and bullets were from a Baikal pistol. Baikals are pretty much the weapon of choice. They are old decommissioned army weapons which are either re-commissioned in Lithuania or Bulgaria and then shipped over, or more likely shipped in and re-commissioned here. They are pretty basic, but that's probably why these street gangsters use them. But they are so stupid. They either buy the guns for a small fortune - anything from £500 to £1,000 depending on the demand - or even worse, hire them out. They don't have a clue about how to look after them. They don't know how to take them apart and clean them, or oil the mechanisms. They wrap them in some oily cloth, then they wonder why they jam or misfire when they use them. I tell you, the amount of jobs that we go to where the gun's misfired or jammed on the second shot you wouldn't believe.

Don't get me wrong, we do get other weapons – Mac 10's, Glocks - but to be honest Baikals and shotguns are the most common. They are cheaper and the ammunition is easier to get hold of. Anyway, although we didn't recover the gun at the scene, we knew what we were looking for. The retrieved bullets - the one in the door frame and the one that was still in Bakara - also gave us a pretty good idea that the weapon had been used in a shooting in North London.

We didn't get much out of Bakara. He was in a bad way after the incident and the paramedics did a good job just keeping him alive. To be honest with you, I knew he wouldn't make it. I read the police intel reports which described his injuries as life threatening. He had two gunshot wounds. The one in his shoulder wasn't so bad but the one in his abdomen had ruptured his liver. Once I knew that it was pretty obvious that at best his injuries would be permanently life changing and at worst he wouldn't make it through.

I had officers at the hospital trying to question him from the off, but he was in too bad a shape. The next best thing was to focus on the technological forensics - the phone, laptops, and social media. We went to Bakara's home address and seized his laptop and computer. His brother was less than pleased I seem to recall because he had course work on it, but to be honest that's the least of our concerns.

We already knew a lot about Bakara from our intelligence and association charts. We had him linked to known members of the PYG, a group of street drug dealers who had built up a reputation for violence and intimidation. They had been a perennial nuisance for some time, involved in anything from anti-social behaviour to some pretty brutal beatings. One fireworks night they managed to close off part of Peckham Road by throwing rockets from one of the high rise blocks.

Bakara was always there or thereabouts. He wasn't one of the ring leaders, but he was always on the fringes and was a known associate of Andre Reid, who was a well-known older. Reid had a street name of "Psychs" and had a history of robbery, class A supply, firearms and serious violence. The intelligence told us that Bakara and members of his crew had a big fall out with one of the ring leaders, Samuel Ojafutu, known as "Sizer". Ojafutu was a violent psychopath and he and KJ Adekoya, another one of the gang, had started up their own drug chain down to the West Country. We had already worked with Avon and Somerset Police on a test purchase operation, so we had a pretty good knowledge of Reid, Ojafutu and Adekoya's movements.

What the technological forensics told us was the extent of the fall out. Facebook and YouTube is one of the best sources of intelligence. I really don't get it with these kids, you know. They don't want to talk to us, but they leave giant size footprints over social media, telling us who's linked with who, who's fallen out and who's after taking a chunk out of someone.

But the best piece of technological forensics is mobiles. Nowadays we get more intelligence from mobiles than anything else. Not only can we get infinite detail of who has contacted who, but we can also pin point with absolute accuracy, a mobile phone to a location, at any time and within a couple of metres.

We had Bakara's phone and we had Reid's phone. Working through them we were able to accurately pin point Ojafutu and Adekoya to the location. From an eye witness outside of the block we knew that there must have been at least one or two other people on the scene. We set the team on researching all of the telephone and text numbers in their mobiles. Meanwhile, we obtained search warrants for the suspect's two home addresses and arrest warrants. We didn't turn over much from Ojafutu's address. His mum was very aggressive and non-cooperative; she refused to tell us where he was, even though we threatened her with arrest for perverting the course of justice. Having done a detailed search of the home address, one of the officers found a key to a lock up. It was a piece of luck really. When we visited the address we found a padded black jacket stuffed in a bin bag, hidden inside an old carpet. We sent it off for forensics and it revealed gun-shot residue on the sleeve.

Adekoya was slightly easier. The eye witness said that one of the assailants was wearing distinctive red trainers; you know the type, like Vans. As luck would have it, there was a pair in a bag at his home address. I remember his house really well, it was a mess and I recall thinking that the trainers were probably the most expensive thing Adekoya owned, so he couldn't throw them away. The shoes had blood in the fabric and on the sole which matched Bakara's and Richards'.

We also put covert surveillance on Reid. My experience told me that Reid was involved somehow. We'd been after him for years and we were really keen to finally nail him. So we set up a 24/7 surveillance; got a really good observation point from a council flat. As luck would have it, we observed him moving a small bundle from a bin chute into a drain pipe. The team moved in and we found the gun. The boost that the arrest gave the team was enormous. We had finally nailed Reid, and this time we knew we had him bang to rights.

The gun was sent off, but we already knew it was the weapon from the shooting. You get these gut feelings. The ballistic forensics confirmed it and the residue on Ojafutu's jacket matched the weapon as well.

So we had Reid, Adekoya and Ojafutu bagged, but there were two things that we needed most. One - we knew there were at least three others at the scene of the crime. Two - we needed eye witnesses, people from the community who saw the group and could pick them out or who saw them fleeing the scene.

We held an anniversary re-enactment of the event a week after the shooting. It's standard practice now to hold a re-enactment to try and encourage people to come forward. We also held a public meeting a few days after that. They are very helpful for us, not that we can say much at them, but we do get a good public turn out, and in this case the local MP turned up, which gave a boost to the troops. The event was full of local residents - mainly elderly, some families, and mums with kids. It's a good way to reassure the community and build some links, even identify a few people who can become sources. Also, we can always highlight a few ways that the council and developers could do more security and designing out crime improvements, rather than leaving it all to the police. Some estates like Bakara's seem to be built to make our life harder, with all the exits and gangways; it's a nightmare.

What I don't really get is the fact that, despite our best efforts, we rarely get people from the community who come forward as witnesses. I'm not naïve enough to realise that the intimidation that local people can feel isn't a big factor, but we can protect people. The truth is that Trident is there to protect them from some pretty serious individuals. The quicker we take them off the streets the better, before another young person gets hurt.

Bakara's case was a pretty low point for us because about a month in we started getting these leaflets sent out around the local area, telling people not to snitch to Trident. They accused us of letting witnesses down and not protecting them. It was pretty damaging and the troops didn't take it well.

Despite this, we still had a few good leads. We came across some CCTV evidence from the garage across the road. It gave us some pretty good images of three people running across the forecourt and through into the newly built North Peckham Estate. The images showed some distinctive clothing including a jacket just like Ojafutu's and red trainers like Adekoya's. We got a witness statement from the attendant but not enough to properly I.D them.

Whilst all this was going on, we put some real pressure on Richards. We knew he was scared, but we made it pretty clear that we knew he was involved in the group and that without anything concrete, we would look to charge him with joint enterprise. His mum was very co-operative, and after we agreed to move her and the family, she helped persuade her son to give us a full statement. He told us Ojafutu and Adekoya were there and he gave us some insights about another one of the gang - Timi Obeseymi.

Obeseymi was one of the known associates of Bakara, Ojafutu and Adekoya. Smart, he always one step ahead, but he was always on the edge of everything that was going on, but we never had enough to pin anything on him. However Bakara's phone gave us a couple of telephone numbers that were directly linked to the scene and some texts encouraging Bakara to meet up. We were pretty certain that one of the numbers was Obeseymi's, because a previous investigation some six months earlier had linked it to him.

What Richards told us was that the block was really dark; he arrived late and made his way up to the eleventh floor. The lights on the landing were out but the moment he got up there he saw the flash from a gun, then he was rushed. He said that for a brief moment he saw Bakara and Adekoya, but just the outline of one other person. When he was rushed, he was certain that there were three of them. He wasn't certain who it was but, put two and two together, the phones, the associations and Obeseymi was a prime candidate.

We took a punt and pulled him in. We knew the phone gave us a pretty accurate picture, and that whoever had it in their possession was either at, or very close to, the scene. The combination of the CCTV and Richards' statement wasn't good enough on its own, but based on his associations, if we could get a witness statement, we stood a chance of pinning him down.

I have to say, of all of the suspects Obeseymi was the one that I took an instant dislike to. He was clearly a smart cookie; well educated, but pretty manipulative. He never said a single word throughout all of the interviews. I reckoned he knew we didn't quite have enough, but his silence told me that he was there, at the scene. He might not have pulled the trigger, but he was definitely there. He had every chance of professing his innocence, but never did. He made some allegation that officers abused him, just to divert attention away from him.

The only chance to nail him was the one eye witness who had come forward and saw the group running from the block. We pulled Obeseymi back in for an I.D parade. The eye witness identified him. Not the first time, but it was an ident. But to be honest it was shaky.

The case had been running for over four months now and I was getting heat from above to come up with a result. We'd had a lot of murders recently that hadn't got anywhere, and the no snitching leaflets had caused waves at senior level.

I met with the CPS and ran through the case and evidence. To cut a long story short, we took the decision to run with all four of them. Reid, Ojafutu and Adekoya were pretty much in the bag, and if the judge saw things our way, we had a chance of bagging Obeseymi as well.

I knew we still had one outstanding, but we had absolutely nothing on the final person. What we hoped was that by taking out the others, it might expose him and he'd end up being targeted or looking for revenge.

The job's non-stop, so the next few months were frantic. We had three other reactive cases on the go, as well as a whole pile of new initiatives from above. They call them 'show of strength' days when we go out and hit a number of addresses or carry out weapon sweeps to flush out guns and knives. They serve a purpose, but they take us away from the day job, and with the staffing levels at the moment they are an unnecessary distraction.

We worked with the CPS and pulled the files, evidence and witnesses. The garage attendant was pretty wobbly about giving evidence. It appears that some boys had been over and threatened him and other members of staff. We had to arrange with his bosses to move him and put some protection in at his home, but he still wasn't happy.

The trial was scheduled for 6 weeks. I got bad vibes about it from day one, because I know the judge and I had already had one run in with him on a previous case. He clearly took the side of the defendants and gave us a really rough ride. All the boys had pretty good briefs, but we had enough watertight forensics on Ojafutu and Adekoya to get a solid conviction. Reid we knew we had in the bag.

But Obeseymi was always going to be more difficult and I knew the moment his barrister started questioning the forensic expert that that we were in trouble. What I wasn't expecting was the ferocity of attack by the judge for bringing him to trial, and the formal complaints that he made against the CPS and the lead investigator - me. The head of the CPS complained to the head of Trident and I got hauled in. I got my balls chewed over it, but the boss knew the reasons why we had gone for it and at the end of the day, that's part of the job.

The others were all found guilty and the sentences were a good result. We took three pretty nasty individuals off the street for a long time, which protects the community. As far as Obeseymi goes, we will just have to bide our time. We will get him, I've know doubts about it. We keep close tabs on him and know his associates and movements. The time will come; he will make a stupid mistake, and when he does we will do a proper job on him.

I know what you're going to say. What about the other person? We still don't have a lot on them yet. I can't say much because we are still investigating, but we have a pretty good idea who the fourth suspect is. We have just never had enough on them to bring it to an arrest; I'm not sure we ever will. Since the trial, the team has been moved around and my team is now part of SCD1 - the murder squad. We've got a lot to learn. Most of us haven't done proactive work for a long time, so it's going to be a tough few months, and the chances of pulling out old cases is pretty remote. But if the evidence comes forward, or we get lucky on some intel, then we will pick it up. When it happens, it will be pretty tough for all those involved, but we have a duty to bring people to justice, regardless of who it is or how long it takes.

That's a really good question - "What do I really think happened that night?"

What the intel tells me is this: there was an argument between the group. We may never know what it was over, but the YouTube and Facebook postings show a big fall out between Bakara, Ojafuto and Obeseymi. I would put money on it that Ojafutu hired the gun from Reid. Ojafutu started sending out messages to get Bakara onto the eleventh floor of the block. When Ojafutu turned up along with Adekoya, he went up to the eleventh floor to wait out for Bakara. He got Obeseymi send Bakara up there on the pretext he was meeting his girlfriend. I would put money on the fact that the fourth person was already hiding in the block on one of the lower floors with the gun that Ojafutu had given him. Bakara arrived just a few minutes later and Obeseymi made sure he went up to the eleventh floor. I am convinced that Obeseymi was at the scene. Ive no evidence but its my gut reaction and my gut reaction is rarely wrong.

Ojafutu and Adekoya had killed the lights because they intended to knife Bakara. Stabbing someone was much more Ojafutu's MO - close and personal. The killer arrived at the scene a few seconds behind Bakara. He could hear a fight ensuing and fired the gun.

Richards got to hear about the set up, but arrived too late. The boys rushed him and either Adekoya or Ojafutu stabbed him on the way out. We never recovered the knife, so we could never be certain which one it was. Obeseymi was a party to it. Ive got no concrete evidence by he was a party, end of.

The most salient point is that I am convinced the killer didn't intend to shoot Bakara. The target was Ojafutu.

Bakara's biggest mistake was getting involved in such a low life bunch as this lot. As I said, the best thing the police can do is take as many of them off the streets as we can. The more we lock up, the more chance we have of stopping these senseless killings and protecting the law abiding community.

I can't think of a more important job than that.

Chapter 12
The Killer's Story Part 1

I didn't mean to kill him.

It was dark and I couldn't see. I could hear the noises and I thought I caught a flash of Samuel's jacket. I heard his voice so I fired. The gun jammed so I fired again and it kicked back in my hand.

There was screaming and people running and I just ran hard, man, hard as I could. I was real scared. I don't rightly remember what happened to the gun, I just ran.

I was scared. I never meant to shoot Anton. It was Samuel, never Anton.

Chapter 13
Money Talks

For each of the characters set out in these pages, the recognition of their cultural identity and the yearning for social acceptance and aspiration is real. For each of them they have had to face the challenges of emotional trauma. For some, those challenges are heaped upon them until they crack, and for others they see it through the eyes of their profession - a police officer, judge, teacher or surgeon - seeking solutions in the lives of those that come before them.

But in a society where 'what we have', rather than 'who we are', can be as big, or even a bigger recognition of success, having 'stuff' - the right stuff - really matters.

One of the biggest challenges is putting ourselves in the shoes of another person; seeing the world through their eyes; experiencing their childhood, their perceptions of fairness or unjust treatment; measuring progress based on their sense of achievement, not ours. When you grow up in a family who are struggling just to survive, providing anything that is beyond the basics can seem like a chasm. That does not just mean the essentials in life - light, heat and food - it also means the emotional basics. There is not the time or space to nurture, just enough to lecture "don't do this," "make sure you do that," "sort this out." The pressure of 'just managing' means that relationships do not get formed, and when there are those few special moments, the lack of familiarity between mum and son or sister and brother creates an awkwardness which stifles honest emotional dialogue.

Solace for many young adolescents is found in their peer groups. Just like Darrell, Samuel, KJ, Timi and Michael found it in theirs, through youth clubs, football, basketball or the gym, through music, school and college.

But wanting to belong has its own pressures. Having the right trainers, or the right jacket, having the right sports kit and no 'hand me downs' from your older brother or cousin, is just as important as the social, or emotional, connections between people. When you are in a group you do not want the right stuff to stand out, you want it to blend in. The right gear is the visual façade that helps hide away your emotional fragility. Stuff really matters.

So here is the scenario relayed by a gang member, that I worked with, about his early life. When he was 10 or 11 he was friends with a group who used to tease him about his trousers being short and that his trainers were from the market.

So he went to his mum and said, "Mum can I have a new pair of trainers?"

His mum said "No."

That's it. Just, "No."

So he said, "Mum I want a new pair of trainers 'cos da boys keep giving me a hard time and said I can't be their friend, 'cos I look like a hobo."

And his mum said, "No. Boy stop your whingin' and whinin' 'bout shoes that gonna not fit you in 5 minutes." She cussed him and gave him a slap for good measure.

He never asked her again. But he went to school and threatened some boys for their lunch money and bought the trainers. So his mum would not know, he kept them hidden outside of the flat.

The next time he wanted some new trousers he robbed someone on the way home. He found that committing crime a second time was not as difficult as the first, nor was the third or the sixth or the twelfth. Once he had a reputation, some of the olders got him into couriering, then supplying. It was easy; he had rep and was expendable. After a while he stopped hiding stuff from this mum. He never lied to her about what he was doing, because she never asked him any questions. Every now and then he bought stuff for the house; after all he couldn't have his mates round playing X-Box on a small screen TV, when 42 inch plasmas were the rage.

When he was finally arrested and sentenced his mum described him as a good boy who never placed undue demands on her.

What he told me about the start to his criminal life was quite profound. He said that it was not that his mum said "No" that was the issue for him. He knew that life was hard, that they did not have much money. He knew that she was working double shifts and that sometimes she went without meals so she could pay the bills. He knew his mum loved him. But he was 10 going on 11. He had never asked her for anything before, and this really mattered. Those trainers really, really mattered. He was going to go to big school and he was frightened because he heard that little kids got beaten up at big school and if he did not have any trainers his friends were not going to be his friends, and he was going to be going to big school all alone with no one to protect him and he was scared.

It was not that she said no, it was that "no" was all she said. There was no explanation; there was no opportunity for dialogue or debate. She said no and she cussed him. There was no room for discussion and as a result, his assessment was that he could never ask again. So he did what he had to do and kept on doing it.

Andre's story is different. He and his brother lived in squalor and chaos throughout most of their early lives. For them having the best brand in clothes, mobiles, game consoles and a roll of money in their pockets was a statement. It told all of their associates that, come what may, they had succeeded, that they had the ability to get whatever they desired and nothing would get in their way. The 'stuff' had no value to them. They got what they wanted and moved on to the next thing just as quickly. It only became of value if someone tried to take it away. Then it had a value a hundred times greater than its monetary worth; a value that could only be met through summary retribution.

We live in a society where we are encouraged to aspire and set high moral and social values in achieving those aspirations. Part of the success is the journey that people go on, and that journey, we are told, will bring us to a point of personal and emotional maturity. The moral compass that the judge referred to so often is the journey, not the destination. Having the educational support, gaining employment, moving on and continually striving is the journey. Having a better house or car, or washing machine, holiday or TV is all part of an indicator of success. These material values are not about 'keeping up with the Jones'', they are about showing that you are still on the journey, that you still have something to aim for, that you aspire for something greater.

But materialism is not the same for Samuel and Timi and Andre. The world has moved on fast in the last decade. For them the material world is weaved in with how their life is lived, how they portray themselves and how they communicate with people. Linking with friends is done through BB's, texts, Facebook, What's App. You have to have the right mobile, the best mobile, a tablet or mini to do that. You can play games on consoles even if your crew is somewhere else. Your life can be run through a tiny electronic device in your pocket, if it is the right device and it is the latest device.

Let us look at Timi - a highly intelligent aspiring young man. He is manipulative, using his intelligence to interrelate and manoeuvre between people, conflicts and feuds, avoiding inquisitive minds and links that would result in his name being called. He did this not by standing out, but by using technology - texting messages of support, words of wisdom, quietly smoothing out personal conflicts and deflecting beef on to others and away from himself. He knew the power and value of technology in terms of group and personal conflict. For him materialism gained by the power of communication, of networking, building your social value, was never just a part of a journey, it was the passport to a new life.

Materialism - the right stuff - for many young people is their life. In the world that they are growing up in, being robbed of your mobile is not just about losing a piece of electronics. That mobile holds every link and contact that you have; every number for your friends and family. It is not the inconvenience factor that is the issue, it is that it is immensely personal, It links you to everything important in your life and everything that protects you in your life. Not being in contact, not being able to link in with the daily chat, noise and activity is like being isolated and cut out. It is like the whole world is moving around you at high speed and you are left standing still trying to catch attention but being ignored. And the worse thing for many of the young people whose lives are on these pages, is that not being included, being left out of things is the biggest fear. It is the fear of being out on your own. It is the fear that in that quiet space, all of your personal fragility, self-doubts, emotional inadequacies that have burdened you for your whole life, will come to the fore - exposing the feelings of personal worthlessness and paranoia that you have, allowing them to seep to the surface, exposing the vulnerability that you have been hiding away for so many years.

No, having the right stuff is not about materialism – it is about life. This is the reason why materialism is the fourth of our 5 dynamic factors.
For many young people materialism is the here and now. Darell did everything he could to blend in with the group, because of fear. An essential part of the blending in was to have the right stuff. Samuel's desire for material possession was status and an ongoing competition with Anton and Timi to be seen to be one step ahead. He knew he did not have the intelligence, but with the best clothes and latest gear, he could take on the persona of the big man. Waiting was not an option, because to wait is a small sign of weakness that can be exploited by those who are seeking any chink they can use to exert their power and assertion.

There is another aspect to materialism which also defines the lives of those characters that come from areas like Peckham. Parents and elders recognise that sticking with Peckham is about recognising that the services, support and businesses that surround them have been established through the demands that they, as a community, have demanded. The shops do not stock things because they think they are great products, they stock them because they are products that will sell. It is no different for the plethora of children centres, family support clubs, faith groups, social clubs and health agencies. There is a demand and for second, third and fourth generation families, they have established their own network of support and self-help. You can walk into a flat on the Friary and find a group of women filling the sitting room and providing an unbreakable bond of support and help.

But for the most recent generation they have been told to aspire, to use education to forge a new path and achieve new goals. After all, we are in an age of technological revolution which brings the world to our doorstep. Poignantly, success is summed up in the story of KJ's sisters. They worked hard, stuck to their goals and got the careers they had strived for.

Then what? They moved out. They used their achievements to get a new life in a new area. They talk about their lives not in terms of what Peckham helped them become, but as a testament to their resilience; that despite growing up in Peckham they "made good."

So, if aspiring means moving on, what happens to those that do not have the ability, or family support, or connections, to aspire? What happens to the KJ's, Samuel's and Andre's in Peckham? They do not have a father figure who can inspire just by the way he goes out every day and works hard for his family. They do not have a male role model who they can sit down with and just talk about the knocks in life and how it strengthens your resolve, rather than breaking you up. Society is a rough place when you have no education, no job prospects, no money and what you see around you every day are people struggling with no job, no money and no prospects.

Social injustice is written large on every street corner for these young people, because they see those that aspire move out and do not get left behind. That is what the competitive, fast moving, high tech society that they see tells them. They do not get good grades and they see their opportunities shrinking all around them. They apply for jobs that they never get an interview for and they get sent on apprenticeship courses that just about covers their travel. What they do know is that there is another alternative. It has risks, but to start with the risks are part of the attraction. As Andre said, the adrenalin rush is a way of remembering you are alive. You can turn over a few hundred a day running drugs; even more by hustling. The current phrase is "work", selling "food", or moving on to couriering weapons, extortion, kidnap, rape, or retribution through violence.

For those that do not have the support to aspire in society, a society that seems to reinforce their injustice, there is another society, a society of drug dealing, violence and sexual exploitation. A society which has targets and goals, high aspirations, high risks for unattainable high rewards at the highest of price - your life.

So, for many young people, having money and having the right "stuff" goes some way to addressing the daily experiences of social injustice, proving they can aspire to the good things in life, whatever the cost and through whatever means. The value of life is cheap because they do not value theirs, but they do value who they are today, what they have today and not who they want to be tomorrow. So many of the stories of those young adults caught up in gang violence talk about surviving each day - "When I get up, I do what I need to do to survive the day, end of."

Of all the characters that you will meet, it is the judge whose assessment is the most profound. He is right that social injustice creates an environment where the moral compass of many of the young people that end up incarcerated, is diverted by personal or monetary gain.

But when you have grown up in a world of violence, where fear is a constant, where you are physiologically and emotionally attuned to react to threats as part of your self-defence mechanism, where you have no father to protect you, no one to guide you, where what you possess today means everything because tomorrow is too far away to contemplate, where the adult world around you seems to socially reject you - resolving conflict through dialogue will never be an option. Get what you need and protect what you have by whatever means, because at least having the right clothes and with the right stuff you are visibly acceptable and technologically connected, even if you feel emotionally isolated.

Yes, stuff matters.

Chapter 14
A Father's Story

I don't know what you are doing comin' round here knockin' at my door.

No, you can't come in.

What lies has that good for nothing boy been tellin' you about me? S'pose he say I beat him day an' night. That boy needed some harsh punishment to knock him into shape and no man died from a little beatin'. Lord knows if I had been around to beat him hard he would not have brought down all this shame on his family. You people comin' around telling me how to deal with my boys, what message you think you are giving dees youths. You are da ones putting all of dem thoughts into their heads about what is right and what is wrong.

No, I haven't seen him for long time. That mother of his always givin', givin', makin' him into a spoilt boy wantin' more. You think I'm hangin' around, I got pressin' things to do, I'm a respectable man, look at me, I have an important job with lots of responsibility. You think that I have time for all that nonsense.

Go away and leave me and my family in peace. I have enough to deal with without all of this stupidness bein' brought to me door.

Now go away.

Chapter 15
A Surgeon's Story

My father was a respectable man. He was a lawyer and had his own practice. My mother, she was a top personal secretary, working for an international company. We had a good life in Nigeria, a big house with a pool, nice cars. My father was a very important man.

My father knew the value of a good education and how important it was for his children to have a proper English education. When I was 10 and my sister was 8 my father brought us to England. He gave up his business and home for his children. He sacrificed everything so we could have the best chance. We moved to a place called Stoke Newington in Hackney. It was hard for us because we had everything back home and then we were in a small house and tiny garden. But my father told me about the importance of knowledge and that I should strive to learn and learn to achieve. That was my father's message every day, to strive to learn and learn to achieve. Here, I had it inscribed in this frame so that when I look at it I would remember my father and his strength of conviction.

Yes, it was very hard. My mother couldn't get a job as a secretary, so she took up cleaning work to make sure we had money. After 3 years she had moved on to administration, working for the same firm. She was very organised. At home and at work, she knew where everything was and had everything in its place. She was a good woman who believed in right from wrong. My father couldn't get a job as a lawyer. He applied for job after job, but none of the firms would take him. They said he didn't know the English law, or he wasn't qualified enough. He never said, but I know he thought that it was because he was black.

You must remember that this was the late 1970's. Margaret Thatcher had just become prime minister; the country had many problems. Things were very different back then for a black man. An educated black man was a person to fear. There is prejudice and discrimination nowadays but back then it was very much worse. It wasn't good enough to be a good black lawyer then, you had to be the best lawyer, if you were to be accepted as being black.

My father studied hard and started a law degree at night school. But he needed to work. My father is a very proud man. He wouldn't take any money from the government when he said he could work. So after a year he got a job as a housing officer for the local council. He worked at an office in Stoke Newington. They paid good money and he helped lots of people on the estates that he managed. My father took his responsibility most seriously and the people he looked after respected him. Sometimes when we went to the local supermarket he would be stopped by people who would ask him lots of questions and shake his hand.

Every now and then my father would fly back to Nigeria to oversee our house, or to do some legal work. There were still clients in Lagos who wanted to use my father's services, even though he had closed his practice. He had a number of business clients who had big import and export trades; big business men who needed the best lawyers, and were willing to pay top dollar for my father.

So, four of five times a year he would go home. We could not sell our house. There were rules about the money we could take out of Nigeria and my father said that the government would take all of the money for the house. So we let it out to family, aunts or uncles. My father was always very careful and made sure he kept a close eye on what was happening back home.

My home life was good. My parents worked hard and made sure me and my sister went to a good school. Our primary school was a church school - St Matthias - and the teachers were good people. I was bright and my mother would give us lessons at home to make sure we were always studying hard. Every Saturday morning she would sit us down and we would do mathematics or English. We would not stop until lunchtime and if we did not do well, she would make us work in the afternoon. On Sundays we would all go to church and in the afternoon go to visit friend's houses or sometime go to Clissold Park. Some days, when we had studied hard or done well in an exam we would go to one of the museums like the Natural History Museum or the Science Museum.

My parents kept us busy. They made certain that there was no time for playing out in the streets. If we had friends they were from church or cousins. But we never played out. My mother or father always took us to school and always brought us home. They made sure I sat the entrance exam to a private secondary school in Islington and I got in. My sister went to a convent. This was our life. I never questioned my parents. But when I look back I see that my father and mother were protecting us. They gave us the best education to make sure that we could have a proper career with prospects.

Just after I went to sixth from, my father got arrested. He was in Nigeria and the police arrested him. They locked him up for 6 months without a trial. At first, when we didn't hear from him we thought that he had become ill. My mother rang our family and all of the hospitals. After a month we heard from a lawyer friend, telling us that they had come for my father in the night. They had charged him with fraud and conspiracy against the government. My family had to pay a lot of money to get him out. It took a whole year. After 6 months in prison he was released but placed under house arrest. My father gave up the house as a payment to a chief of police and then they let him go.

He didn't tell us what happened to him but when we came back he was very, very thin and he had a deep scar across his face and wounds down his back. My father never went back to Nigeria and cut off all of his business associations. He told me when I was much older that he knew that a cousin had set him up for money from the police. It was very bad.

When did I decide to be a surgeon? I do not remember. But I can tell you that I do not remember a time when I did not want to be a surgeon. When my sister and I were young we would play lots of games. Playing hospitals was my favourite. I would pretend to be the doctor and treat her broken arm or cut head. My parents even bought me a doctor's gown and toy stethoscope.

I studied hard at school. I took four A-Levels - mathematics, chemistry, biology and physics. I knew that to get to medical school I would have to get A's for each subject. I remember how hard it was and how stressful for me and my family. My father was very worried for me. I know that the years of prejudice that he suffered as a professional black man haunted him. He did not want his son to suffer the same fate in a profession that was dominated by white men. The world was changing, but when you experience deep seated prejudice first hand, it is hard to move on.

In 1987 I gained entry to King's College London, a highly reputable medical college. It was 6 years of hard study, before I started as a trainee doctor as part of my foundation course at Chelsea and Westminster Hospital on the Cromwell Road. As a trainee you still continue to study and undertake ward duties working alongside doctors and qualified surgeons. The foundation course took two years. It is not unusual for a trainee doctors and training surgeons to work and study 16 hours a day 7 days a week. There are a series of exams and interviews with the Medical Board. They do this to make sure you have a detailed knowledge of the signs and symptoms and how to treat them. Once my foundation course was completed I then had to undertake a further 3 years learning the range of surgical techniques and specialist areas of surgery.

I had always held a burning ambition to specialise in general surgery, particularly dealing with trauma cases. After 3 years I gained a trainee position with a senior surgeon - Mr Campbell - who acted as my mentor. I assisted him in operations and carrying out surgical procedures. He was a senior surgeon at the hospital's A&E department. Finally, I gained a position as a paid trainee at the Royal London Hospital, where for 6 years I performed surgery alongside the senior Consultant Surgeon Mr Laidlaw, specialising in trauma, specifically gun shot, knife and blunt instrument traumas, such as car accidents. Finally after 18 long years I was fully qualified gaining the Certificate of Completion of Specialist Training and became a fellow of the Royal College of Surgeons in 2005.

It is not easy. I dedicated all of my time to qualify as a doctor and then a surgeon. I refused to let anything change that path. It was more than doing it for myself, that made me so single minded. I wanted to become a surgeon to make my father proud of me, especially after all of the sacrifices that he had made for me and my sister.

It took 18 years for me to become a surgeon. 18 long hard years; for much of that time I could hardly support myself financially. I had little money until I was in my last few years as a paid trainee consultant. There were some days when things went wrong that I wanted to give up, but I could not do that and let my father down, who wanted so much to see me achieve. I got married about three years from the end of training. I was 34. I had known my wife Stella for many years. We went to the same church and had grown up together. But I was very single-minded. I was determined to wait and marry at the right time when I could support my wife independently and not rely on anyone. So we waited a long time. We married in St Matthias Church, Stoke Newington. It was a typical Nigerian wedding with lots of colour and celebrations. Stella is like my mother, a strong independent women; a teacher who has her own career. We have two beautiful daughters, twins, who have just started school, a good private school in Chigwell where we now live and where my father and mother can visit and spend time. I pride myself in the closeness of my family. It is our family that makes us strong.

Let me tell you a little bit about my role as a surgeon here at King's College Hospital. I am the consultant for the Accident and Emergency department. It is one of the busiest departments of its kind in the whole of the country. I can tell you that on average we see around 3,500 patients a year, many of them have injuries related to alcohol consumption and we see a lot of domestic violence cases. We are also the busiest department in London in terms of gun and knife injuries. Last year we dealt with nearly 380 knife and 30 gun-shot victims. It is always around the same number every year, a few less, a few more. Although I think the last year or so it has been not quite so busy. My team and I have become highly specialist in dealing with these types of injuries.

Let me show you around my department. This is the A&E reception and waiting area. A nurse will meet you and take down the information of your injuries or ailments. You will then be directed to reception who will verify your personal details and book you in. Most knife and gun injuries will be brought in by ambulance, but I can tell you that there have been many, many times that a person with a serious wound has arrived at my department on their own, or been driven in by an associate.

This is the treatment areas where we see patients. There are 12 bays and over a weekend they are all in full use. There are times when we do not have enough nurses or doctors to keep up with the demand, but I will tell you that we have become acclimatised to such difficulties. For any patient who is presented at A&E we have three fundamental roles - diagnosis, that is identifying the medical concern; treatment; and the care or well-being of the patient. All three are tied together and require the attention of the staff and consultant surgeon, including knife and gun-shot injuries.

If a knife wound is not severe, we will stabilise the patient in one of these bays prior to surgery. You will know that we never remove the weapon if it is still in the body, but will pack the wound to stem the blood loss. Four or five years ago we had many cases of knife wounds to the back of the legs or buttocks. I am lead to understand that this was because of the view that such injuries were less life threatening and could be seen as a point of status by the assailant over the victim. You must understand however that the thighs and buttocks are made up of a complexity of capillaries, muscle tissues, tendons and arteries. Damage to these intricate areas will cause extensive blood loss and is life threatening. The most common cause of loss of life is blood loss. The normal male body holds 5 litres of blood. A young person of around 13 years of age can hold just over 3 litres. If you lose one litre of blood, that is 20% of the body's total, and a blood loss of greater than 30% can lead to major complications. Over that amount and the body struggles to be able to deal with the loss and starts shutting down as part of its attempt to preserve blood flow to the heart and major organs. The result will be disability or death.

In most cases of a knife or gun-shot injury we see patients who have lost between one and two litres of blood. Our first concern is to increase blood and fluids into the patient and stem the blood flow. Blood is the fluid of life because it is blood that takes the oxygen and nutrients to tissues and the toxic waste away. Once we have achieved this and stabilised the patient we can start preparing for surgery.

We have four operating theatres, two large and two small. The two large ones are new. When I became the consultant surgeon here in 2008 we only had two theatres. This was not adequate for the demand. Now we have the ability to carry life-saving surgery with the best equipment. Here, come inside and look around. I know you will think that it looks a little like a TV set, but this isn't a drama programme. Can you imagine a young teenage boy, scared for his life and being brought into here, surrounded by all of these machines, heart monitors, drips, blood infusions, oxygen and gas and air tubes. We have specialist equipment over here for keyhole surgery and micro surgery, which is vital and has aided us in stemming the internal damage due to knife injuries and the removal of bullets. The least amount of intrusive surgery that we have to undertake, the better chance a patient has of survival. In urgent cases, patients may be brought straight into these theatres. Many of them are screaming with pain and fear. They are young men, really some are still children, and they do not want to die. Some will be crying for their mother, but while we are operating on them in the theatre they are on their own.

Here you see these swabs? Each one holds half a litre of fluid. During surgery we may use 3, 4 or 5 of these swabs just to clear up the blood. Quite often we will have to operate two or three times - first to stop the blood loss; second to repair the wound; and third to undertake further surgery where we are not satisfied that there is not secondary damage. A stab wound to the abdomen could puncture an organ, the spleen or the bowel. We need to assess the extent of the damage. A male will have to have a catheter like this inserted into his penis to remove the urine. I have dealt with many abdomen injuries which require a colostomy bag inserted directly into the abdomen or the upper part of the intestines. We make a small insertion through the wall of the stomach and your side like this and this tube is inserted through there. The tube has to be big enough to remove solids. For some patients the damage to their bowels can be so severe that they have to have a colostomy bag for the rest of their lives. They are strapped to their side and they have to empty them four of five times a day. Do not think this is rare. It is not.

Yes I remember Anton Bakara. I was the on call consultant that evening. I recall that he was unconscious when they brought him in. The ambulance only had half a mile to travel from the scene to the hospital, but the paramedics had to stop twice to perform CPR. He had two bullet entries. The entry wound to the shoulder had passed straight through but had severely damaged the brachial plexus as it travelled through the body. The second was far more concerning. The bullet wound had entered from the right hand side of the torso in the upper part of the chest and travelled through into the right lobe of the liver. The bullet had splintered on entry shattering part of the rib cage, and fragments of the bullet were still wedged in his liver. He had lost over two litres of blood and his body was already shutting down. We couldn't stem the blood loss quickly enough and we used over 5 litres of blood in our attempts to stabilise him.

We packed the shoulder wound and focused on the abdomen, repairing the wound as swiftly as possible. We knew that we would have to carry out a second operation, but removing the fragments of the bullets and attempting to seal the tissue and severed arteries was the priority. Next we carried out surgery to the shoulder, removing the fragmented bone and reducing the blood loss due to the extensive damage to the blood vessels.

The surgery took over five hours. We placed him in a medically induced coma to ensure that the bodies reaction to the injuries were minimised. Our next concern was infection. The injuries that this young man sustained are highly susceptible to infection.

I am afraid that things did not go well for this young man. The combination of high blood loss and the damage to the liver resulted in his body being unable to cope. Such loss also results in low levels of potassium called hypokalaemia, which in turn can lead to organ failure. Potassium is an essential body salt which is vital in the body's fluid balance and nerve function. Low potassium can not only affect the organs such as the heart, but can also affect the patient's immune system making them susceptible to infection, which as I have said, was the case in the types of injuries that he had received.

After four days we were faced with two options. Firstly, we could continue with the induced coma and hope the body would start to recover. However, I saw no signs that this would be the case. My prognosis was that the organs were not strong enough to cope and the sharp drop in potassium appeared to have damaged the heart. Secondly, we could reduce the pressure on the organs, which would require the removal of his limbs, thereby not requiring the organs to work so hard to provide blood oxygen and nutrients to the whole body. You must understand this dilemma, but I am a surgeon and my first aim is to preserve life. Mrs Bakara understood the options and agreed to the surgery. She was a strong woman who put her faith in God and her trust in me.

We amputated his left leg. All surgery has its risks, however the advancements in amputation procedures has been considerable in recent years. One of the few positive outcomes from war is that during conflict surgical advancements are made. Minefields in Africa and improvised explosive devises in Iraq and Afghanistan have provided surgeons the opportunity to make significant progress, using new techniques and technology. I spent a year working as a field surgeon in Sierra Leone, after my final year as an assistant surgeon and experienced these new techniques first hand.

The surgery went smoothly, but I am afraid the young man made no appreciable recovery and at best had stabilised. We were faced with a further choice - to carry out a second amputation or risk organ failure. Mrs Bakara asked me to do everything in my power to save her son. On the Monday we amputated his right leg. I have to be honest with you and say that at this stage I feared that we would not be able to save the boy. This was a final attempt, and such measures are extraordinary. However Mrs Bakara had placed her faith in me and I owed her and her son one last chance.

Despite our best efforts and the prayers of his family, the young man deteriorated. He had fought hard but I must report that by this time the battle was lost. Mrs Bakara was a brave woman. She chose to bring his life to an end in a dignified way and on the Friday we slowly brought him out of the coma and he died peacefully. Mrs Bakara never left his side during the ten days that he was in the Intensive Care Unit. She held her boy at the very end and she and her other son wept as he finally passed away.

Mrs Bakara is a strong woman who has suffered many tragedies in her life. She has a heart the size of a lion and over the past few years we have become close friends, speaking at churches and schools to help other young people understand the consequences of gun and knife crime on innocent families like hers. She has met my wife and family and we have gone to church together on the anniversary of her son's death. She rejoices his life, not his death, but I know there are days when she suffers and the tears roll down her cheeks and she finds it hard to move forward. But she is strong and she has the love of her son, her friends and family. I am not sure I would have the strength to deal with such a tragedy and I believe we are indebted to people like Mrs Bakara who, despite all that she has suffered, still has faith in humanity.

What is my message? Life is precious. It is not something that should be squandered away on some petty feud or argument. Taking a life is a sin in God's eyes, regardless of which God you believe in or which religion you follow. I am a son, a father, a brother and a surgeon and in every walk of my life I believe in the sanctity of life. I could not save Anton Bakara's life. Whenever I am faced with the prospect that despite my best endeavours I cannot save a patient, I feel particularly depressed, and in this case it was a real personal blow. Here was a young man starting out on his journey to becoming an adult, a young man with ambitions and prospects. I saw in him something of me at his age, a young black man wanting to make his parents proud and with the world ahead of him.

I recall going and talking to my father about the case. He is 68 now, still helping people out in the community at the Citizens Advice Bureau and the church. We sat on a bench in Clissold Park near the Tennis Courts just taking in life. I remember very clearly the words that he said to me. He said: "Son, life is not always measured on how much you succeed. Sometimes it is measured on what you learn from failure that makes you a greater man."

I have chosen a profession where on many occasions the balance of life and death is in the hands of me and my team. I believe that it is medical advancements that have given the surgeon an advantage; our skills are preventing more young men being saved from gun and knife trauma than at any other time.

I continue to strive to learn and learn to achieve.

But I am a surgeon. I do not deal with the mind. I cannot understand why a young person would - with full knowledge of the impact - go out and shoot another person with the full intent of killing him. There is much in society that I do not understand, but what I cannot grasp is why a young person would place so little value in a human life and so little regard for the families who suffer when their most precious possession - their child - is taken from them. A surgeon cannot cut out this cancer that is eating away at our society. If only we could.

Chapter 16
KJ's Story

He raped me. He came into my room; he stroked my hair and asked if I knew how much he loved me. He stank of alcohol and I could tell he'd been smoking weed. I felt his hand go under the bed cover. He was stroking my back and I thought he was just comforting me, like he usually did. Then his hands pushed down the back of my shorts. I struggled, I struggled real hard, but he was a strong man and he pushed me face down into the pillow so I couldn't breathe. I felt this burning between my buttocks and he raped me.

From that day on he stopped being my dad. I was 6. I was too frightened to tell mum. He beat her real bad. I think she knew what he did to me because after that day he left. Mum said he wanted to keep in contact with me. I told her no. She said he would come round and pick me up. I packed a bag and sat on the front step. I swore that if I saw his car I would run away. When he didn't show I ran to my room and cried with relief.

I had nightmares.

I would wake up screaming. I wet the bed. Mum took me to the church. The Pastor stripped me naked. He poured palm oil and ground scotch bonnet pepper down my throat until I choked. He put pepper in my eyes and it burnt like hot needles. He struck me with a JuJu stick and lay hands on me. Mum took me to the Pastor several times. He gave me a bracelet to wear to protect me. He put a ring round my leg to keep out the bad spirits.

I tried not to sleep. I learnt to wake up when I could feel the nightmares come.

My father raped me.

I was told I was never to talk about. It would bring shame on the family.

Words mean nothing compared to actions.

I went to school.

I couldn't concentrate.

The teachers said I was a slow learner.

I wasn't. I learnt fast.

I learnt to hide.

She was the most important person. She meant everything to me. But however hard I tried to please her she shunned me. I thought she blamed me for him leaving us. When mum got ill I blamed myself. I thought God was punishing her because of me; what I let him do to me. If I saw my father in the street I would stare at him. I wanted him to feel my hate. He just turned away.

I hate myself the most. What I hate is that I am nothing. I don't feel anything. I don't care. I survive every day, day by day. I linked with people on the street. I wasn't frightened of them. To be frightened you have to have something to lose.

Silent Voices

We did stuff. That's it. We just did stuff. We hung out, we smoked, we did some madness. So what? Home was a hell. Mum was dying and she never had time for me. The house was never a home; it was a filthy shit hole. The carpets were rotting; they smelt of piss. The curtains were nailed up. There was never any food. No one cooked. I ate takeaways, chicken and chips, café or my cultural food from 801, whatever. That's the only thing I miss in here; proper African food.

I was 15.

I was still sleeping in the same bed he raped me in.

At home I was in the way. When I was in she called me lazy, when I was out she said I was up to no good; I stayed out.

Samuel and I did some dealing. We made some money. We weren't the only ones. Back in the day all the kids did it. We got noticed 'cos we were more forceful. We just got on with it. We supplied and we delivered. We earned money, it wasn't much. I didn't do it for the money. It kept my mind occupied. I didn't have to think about stuff. That's it.

Anton got in the way. You think I was angry with him? You need to listen. I didn't feel anything. He just got in the way. He did a deal and got it wrong. He lost money. We all know the price when you lose money. He didn't pay up so Samuel and I called his name. If I had seen him I would have shanked him. The debt got settled. It didn't matter how. I'm telling you I really didn't care.

When I got shot it was a relief. It was the first time I felt something since I was 6. I liked the pain. I didn't want it to go away.

Who shot me? I don't know. If I did, you think I'm gonna tell you?

They sent me home. I hated it. I was in a prison inside a prison. I played computer games so I didn't have to think. I smoked weed to numb my brain. I smoked plenty; a bag a day, sometimes more. So what? You don't know what it's like, surviving every day. You have things to mark time. I mark time by surviving. I get up, play x-box, smoke, go out to work, earn food, go to bed. Another day survived.

The worst thing happened. My dad came round; started crying, saying to me he was sorry, said he should have done more for me. If I was stronger I would have wrapped a cord around his neck and choked every inch of life out of him, like he took my life away from me when I was six years old. I never spoke. I sat playing x-box, COD. He came towards me. I turned and faced him. He saw in my eyes what I was thinking. When he left I told him to never come again. I've never seen him since. I smashed up my bed. It was a good feeling.

Anton got shot.

He died.

Samuel thought he was being set up.

We got tipped off by this girl. She hung around the front line. Samuel said he got her to give him head a couple of times. I said we should just rape her. Timi wanted her; raping her would have really got to him. I didn't like Timi. He was too smart. He looked down I me. I knew it was a long way.

We went to the block early. We took out the light bulbs. We heard Anton on the stairs. As soon as he opened the lobby door I grabbed him. Samuel was going to shank him. Then we heard another person. We thought it was Timi. It wasn't.

Samuel pushed Anton towards him and we heard the gun shots. I saw Darell in the lobby. We rushed him and I stabbed him. Samuel and I ran across Peckham Road into Sumner Road. I had blood over my hand. I had cut my finger. I don't rightly know when.

I went home.

Do I like prison? I don't mind. It's got rules. I can live my day by rules. When I got here it was bad. I got raped. I was the new boy. That's what happens. They soon stopped. It's no fun if the person you rape doesn't feel anything. It's like fucking a piece of dead meat.

Timi got raped when he was on remand. He was the wing's sweetheart. He cried and bleated so they raped him more. They got him to suck them off, three or four at a time. He wasn't on my wing but everyone knew. Serves him right. If Samuel got hold of him he'd be dead.

I went to mum's funeral. She wanted me there. They only let me stay for the funeral. It hurt me 'cos I wanted her to see me and talk to me. She didn't even come over.

Wot? You ain't been listening! You people never listen. It was never about my mum, it wasn't her that I wanted to love me. It was my sister, my li'l sister it was always about li'l sister. My mum let me be abused; she knew what he was like. He raped me, he destroyed me and defiled me for the whole of my life and she knew and she did nothing about it, just let it happen, knew it happened and just stood by whilst her six year old son was raped. She was supposed to protect me and she just let it happen. It was my sister that comforted me. She was the only one who cared. Then dad left and my mum fell ill and she blamed me. My sister stopped loving me. Don't you understand? I destroyed everything and I tried to get her to notice me but she stopped seeing me as her brother. She looked straight through me and she cussed me and pushed me away and it hurt so much, for so long, that I stopped caring. And she never comes to see me.

I stopped feeling. I don't give a fuck what happens now, do you get me?

Since I've been inside I've learnt to read; I like reading. I can lose myself when I read; I become someone else. My favourite book is this one - It's called White Fang. I've read it lots. White Fang is a wolf; he's a loner, but a survivor. Here, read this: *"Hated by his kind and by mankind, indomitable, perpetually warred upon and himself waging perpetual war, his development was rapid and one-sided. This was no soil for kindliness and affection to blossom in. Of such things he had not the faintest glimmering. The code he learned was to obey the strong and to oppress the weak.*
He became quicker of movement than the other dogs, swifter of foot, craftier, deadlier, more lithe, more lean with iron like muscle and sinew, more enduring, more cruel, more ferocious, and more intelligent. He had to become all these things, else he would not have held his own nor survive the hostile environment in which he lived."

That's me, White Fang. I am hated and I hate. Most of all I hate what I am.

What will I do when I get out? Survive 'til I die.

Chapter 17
A Judge's Story

I am not sure of your background or the extent of your understanding of the complexities of the criminal judiciary. Let me attempt to lay out the judicial framework that forms the fundamental basis of the English legal system.

As a judge, I am required to adopt a level of impartiality, but that impartiality does not extend to the barristers or legal representatives that present their case at my court. There is a juxtaposition which exists between the impartiality of the court and the bias of the prosecution and defence. The prosecution is required to present their case to prove beyond reasonable doubt that the defendant, and co-defendants in this case, are guilty of the crime that they have been charged. The defence is required to find fundamental flaws in that evidence, either through court process or by providing evidence that brings into dispute the case that the prosecution has put forward.

Despite the courts guidelines and sacrosanct ethical requirements placed on both parties, there is considerable leeway in terms of how the evidence is produced, the lines of questioning and summations which can mislead the court and the jury. Bias exists, and where one party is exerting bias, I, as judge, have to affect redress, which at times negates impartiality.

I can see you are puzzled, so let me give you an example from the very case that you are interested in. The prosecution has brought an eye witness to the stand. They have questioned him and concluded that questioning. The four defendants each had their own barristers and each in turn had the ability to question the witness. One of the barristers - I have forgotten which client he was representing - started to question the eyewitness on his own criminal activity and links to the criminal fraternity. Such questions, designed to discredit the morality of the defendant, holds no place in my court, particularly where the barrister was persistent to the point of bullying. A robust rebuke was required countering the line of questioning and directing the defendant's representatives to refrain from such an approach in future. In summary, impartiality is the position of status quo which requires maintaining and at times redressing. It is a fine line that the jury may not fully appreciate, but is vital in ensuring justice based on the facts, not on speculation.

There are a number of fundamental principles that form the moral and philosophical bedrock of the criminal justice system.

First and foremost - despite views to the contrary - it is government's role to agree legislation, but it is the court, not government, which defines the law. Judges will use the legislative framework to set the context. Judicial guidelines are provided. However, I need to press upon you the importance of the word 'guidelines'. It is case law that formulates the deliberation of the court, and it is case law, not government that ultimately defines the legal boundaries of a sanction in criminal law. In simple terms, case law is the set of existing rulings which have made new interpretations of the law, and therefore can be cited as precedent. The outcome of a case at court sets the precedent for that particular type of case, and thereafter the case or precedent, is referred to in deciding similar cases. I trust that is clear.

Judges and the judicial system is not a whim of government. The courts are independent and will not succumb to the manoeuvrings of party politics. Ministers may wish the courts to do their bidding, but that is not our role. When taking the Judicial Oath, a judge swears "To do right to all manner of people after the laws and usages of this realm without fear or favour, affection or ill will." Bear this in mind and note carefully "without fear or favour". My advice to politicians is to be more diligent in the legislation that they adopt, rather than wasting their time in vain attempts to corral the judiciary, who will wilfully resist such attempts.

Secondly, it is the role of the court, and in particular the judge, to ensure that every aspect of the law is considered. The court cannot be blind to legislation, nor can it allow one piece of legislation the luxury of precedent over another. The legal framework is multi-dimensional and has interconnectivities which create interdependencies. An experienced judge like me has a responsibility to ensure that those presenting the case and those deliberating over the case are cognisant of those interconnectivities.

Again, you seem perplexed by this, so let me explain by way of a simple example. If the police identify a suspect, they have a legal framework in how they can gather evidence to present to the court. The evidence has to be factual, but it also had to be gathered in accordance with the codes and practices laid down through legislation. The 1984 Police and Criminal Evidence Act lays down how the police record their evidence, and case law such as R v Turnbull sets out how the police carry out interviews and record information for evidential purposes. Should the police require evidence to be gathered through covert means, or through the use of undercover Human Intelligence sources, they are required to abide by the legislation set out under the Regulation of Investigatory Powers Act, again defined through case law. Consideration of the defendant's human rights have to be considered under Human Rights legislation and counter balanced against the rights of the victims, their families and community.

It is not uncommon in the criminal court for the judge to enlighten the jury of such interdependencies. Equally, it is not uncommon for the judge to preside over evidence which has been obtained without due diligence to the legislation, and is therefore inadmissible. It is regrettable to say, but the fact is that the most successful defendants are those who focus on the inadequacies of the prosecution case, rather than trying to build their own robust evidence. The police and the Crown Prosecution Service have much to answer on this point.

Thirdly, the principle of morality extends as much to those that administer the court as it does to those who form the defence and prosecution. I recall many years ago that a learned colleague had to adjourn a case when it became abundantly clear that one of the defendants had a close association with his son. His son had a checkered past, and drug related misdemeanours in the West Country had tarnished the reputation of the family - "Ut sementem feceris ita metes." Ten years later, the person charged with Supply of Class A Drugs turned out to be a former university friend of his son, Angus. The family had instigated a lengthy sabbatical for him in southern France. All very hush-hush. The case was reassigned and there were unpleasant rumblings in the chambers for some time. The court of law requires all of its participants to maintain ethical codes and unequivocal transparency. There is no compromise.

Finally, there is no place in the criminal justice system for speculation and assumption. The case must be tried on the facts and the facts alone - "De minimis non curat lex." I can acknowledge the frustrations of the police and the Crown Prosecution Service in gathering the weight of evidence to lay before the court to support their strength of argument. I can equally acknowledge that some of those brought before the court are part of a criminal fraternity bent on violent criminal behaviour. However a court of law is convened to hear the case presented, based on the charges that have been made. The facts are paramount, not the speculation. The jury can take inference from the evidence but they cannot, and must not, make speculation.

I tire of lazy legal representation based on lazy police investigations. Some officers of the Metropolitan Police Service appear to have the supposition that they can convince a jury of a defendant's guilt by laying out a trail of criminal associations to both people and events. None of this evidence bears any relevance to the case in hand. A person's associations are an irrelevance, unless there is clear evidence or inference that those associations meant the person was knowingly involved in the criminal charge laid before the court. Remember, "legum servi sumus ut liberi esse possimus."

The criminal law provides both investigators and barristers with sufficient scope to bring a person before the court where there is evidence of association of that person to a crime. There is an abundance of case law for perjury, perverting the course of justice and aiding and abetting a criminal. Such laws are not new. The concept of joint enterprise is not new either, however some elaboration on joint enterprise might assist you.

Joint enterprise has two interpretations in law. Firstly in tort law, joint enterprise is defined as a business enterprise conducted by several individuals, who each share in the liability arising from their activities. For example - a partnership - where each of the partners have a shared responsibility for the business, in good times and bad. A simple concept, I think you will agree.

Secondly in criminal law, joint enterprise is defined as a conspiracy, or co-operation of two or more individuals to commit a crime. In other words, if your knowledge, actions, or presence leads to a serious crime such as murder, you face the prospect of being charged with murder. Note the fundamental difference here. Whilst in both tort law and criminal law, the parties share responsibility for the outcome, in criminal law your inaction in relation to an event that you know will result in the serious harm of a person or persons, could result in you being presented at my court on charge of murder through joint enterprise.

This does not solely mean that both parties had to be equally involved in the planning and committing of a crime. It is important to understand that where a person agrees to commit a crime with another person, they can then become liable for any other criminal acts by the other person in the course of that criminal venture. In summation, if the three accused went to the scene to assault the deceased and one of the parties pulled a gun and shot him, the other parties could be tried for murder, as principle offenders, through joint enterprise.

The court must determine whether the offender could have anticipated or foreseen what might occur, and the prosecution must bring evidence that proves this beyond reasonable doubt. If the conviction was murder, this would result in a mandatory life sentence. Mere association to a group or gang, without foresight of the intended acts, is insufficient to bring a claim of joint enterprise. Evidence must prevail.

I am sorry, but my time is short and I have another pressing engagement, so let me turn to the trial that you are interested in. The case itself was not unusual. The co-defendants appeared to have little interest in the court proceedings, and one I recall was contemptuous towards the clerks and the bench. I had to warn him and his counsel on several occasions about his attitude. There was nothing distinguishing about them, and their families appeared to have the same contrition that prevails amongst many of the families that fill the public galleries. Perhaps if they had committed the same amount of time and interest with them in their home life, they would have spared themselves the ordeal of this trial and the prospect of a lengthy prison sentence for their sibling.

I had spent many weeks familiarising myself with the evidence that had been lodged, and in particular the police investigation. I was well aware of the shortcomings in some aspects and I looked forward with anticipation the police and expert examination to see how, or indeed whether, those shortcomings would be exposed.

The trail started with the usual formal processes of assigning a jury and swearing them in. A pool of forty potential jurors were narrowed down, partly through their availability for a lengthy trial such as this, but also through the standard questionnaire which verifies the acquaintance or knowledge of any of the parties or witnesses, which is a necessary, if rather perfunctory, procedure. The jurors were sworn in by the clerk. In my address to the jury I reminded them of the importance of confidentiality and silence, but most importantly I stressed the dangers that modern forms of communication such as Facebook and Twitter pose. There was a recent case where a member of the jury was posting highly inappropriate comments on social media, which resulted in proceedings having to be abandoned and a retrial arranged. The cost is substantial and any juror who acts so irresponsibly faces a potential prison term.

The trial opened with the counsel for the prosecution calling their witnesses. I have to express at this point that I was strongly of the opinion that the lead barrister for the prosecution appeared to have made a conscious decision to present the case in a rather anodyne manner. As a result, my interpretation of the evidence presented was that it failed to demonstrate the personal and community impact that such a significant incident would have had.

Contrary to belief, the respective counsels in such cases present an air of mutual respect and decorum towards one another. Whilst the defence solicitors requested a number of in-camera audiences, which resulted in the public gallery being cleared and jury removed, this is not an unusual procedure. There are a number of technical points that counsel may wish to discuss, which need to be undertaken in private, and at times with my guidance.

It is not my role to elicit human emotions, and certainly not to do so in a manner that overrides the evidence that is put before the jury. However, in this case the prosecution failed to produce a single community or family member who could testify as to the impact on them. There was no community impact statement and nothing in the evidence, other than the impersonal statements of professionals who approached the subject with a rather cold, analytical perspective which so often accompanies such specialisms.

In terms of the lead police investigator, I am afraid that this case only reinforced my opinion of him. It is not the first time that he has brought an investigation to my court, and he clearly has a prejudicial view over this stereotypical group of offenders who were presented in the dock. Whilst admittedly, the vast majority of defendants who are brought to trial for these 'gang' killings appear to be young black males, police investigators have a duty to demonstrate that they have pursued their lines of enquiries diligently and with no malice aforethought. In this case, the officer presented evidence that conveyed frustration rather than fact. Admittedly, the evidence on three of the defendants was sound in nature; the fourth was not. The evidence was at best circumstantial and produced an association between the parties, but fell inadequately short of a murder charge through joint enterprise. It did not surprise me that it was leapt upon by the defendant's barrister.

As it unravelled I exercised my judgement and called counsel and the officer to my chambers. I probed the remaining evidence and provided one of my strongest verbal rebukes to the prosecution and the officer, and summarily acquitted the defendant.

The character of the deceased became questionable as the three defence lawyers eruditely set about building the impeccable personas of their clients. These young men became paragons of virtue, staunchly attempting to make the best of their lives, despite the paucity of support and nurturing that most of their peers benefit from.

Two of the remaining three defendants argued self-defence, claiming that the victim had lured them to the location, intent on harming them. The evidence was circumstantial and only supported by both defendants' testimony. I am sure the jury was attuned to the collusion as I was, and my patience wore thin with the rather contemptuous attitude of one of the young men.

Nevertheless, my summing up had to be thorough. I provided the jury with a detailed chronology of the witnesses and their evidence. It is important the each salient point is covered to ensure that the jury fully understands the relevance. As I have said, impartiality prevails, and in summing up I set out the legal framework with respect to the charges and the clear distinction between a charge of murder and a charge of manslaughter. To convict a person of murder the jury must be satisfied that the defendants had clear intent and that their act was premeditated. They must agree that the defendants arrived at the location with a weapon, intent on injuring a person which ultimately led to the loss of life. For a charge of manslaughter, intent does not exist. If the jury were satisfied that the defendants had no intention to harm the victim and the loss of life was a result of a series of unintended consequences, then a charge of manslaughter should be considered.

My summation took one whole day. I am aware that those in the public gallery looked upon the above as rather numbing, but it is important to stress the validity of process if due diligence and fairness is to prevail.

On retiring, I presented the jury with a simple flow chart to aid them in their decisions. It is a customary approach given the consequences of one decision has an impact on the next. Ultimately the jury retired for only a few hours and returned a verdict of guilty of murder on two of the defendants and guilty of possession of a firearm on the remaining individual. All three were sentenced accordingly.

My summary of the four accused is that, like many similar cases, it was abundantly clear that the defendants were neither erudite nor socially integrated. This is not unusual. I have had the misfortune of overseeing a number of similar murder cases, and my overriding assessment is that there are deep sociological and psychological challenges which are fragmenting our society. These young men are distinct from society; a decision that they have consciously taken themselves. In doing so, they have created their own perverse judicial framework containing none of the egalitarian approaches - which, as I have described - are a cornerstone of the British justice system. They lack a sense of any moral compass; a sad reflection on society and the family context from which they originate. It appears to me that this stems from neglectful parenting. The common factor in every case that I have presided over is not colour or faith, but deprivation. The denominator is a lack of a stable family home, the lack of financial stability, and as a consequence ones moral compass is replaced by emotional and financial necessity.

I am ultimately a pragmatist, and pragmatically the lifestyle of which I have had the fortune bears no resemblance to that of the defendants that I am describing. My father was a successful banker and my mother provided a stable home environment. Our family home was on the Surrey Hampshire borders in Grayshott, and we had a small holiday home in the south of France. My brother is a vice president for Proctor and Gamble and I had the support to set my goal on the legal profession early on.

I make no apology for my home life and upbringing, but would ask you to recognise that privilege in one's childhood does not relate to the adult world, where hard work and dedication prevail. I resolutely hold to this opinion and refute the rather truculent view that opportunity is restricted for those in more socially challenged areas. With hard work and dedication to your profession you can achieve your ambitions, and there are many examples in my chambers of people from deprived areas who have achieved their goals. Equally, there are those from stable home environments who commit crime and come before the court.

The fact that I chose my career path at an early juncture in my life and that I had a stable home life, does not mean that I had a smooth journey. My predicted matriculation results at grammar school were not outstanding. I had to knuckle down to achieve the entry level grades for university, and had to have a home tutor for some months to achieve the academic standards that I needed for a good college. I was acutely aware at the time that to become a successful barrister required the hallmark of a recognised university. I gained an offer and finally the grades for a place at Trinity College, Cambridge and completed my four year law degree with honours. I undertook three mini pupilages and applied through the Bar Standards Board before I was finally accepted for a one year pupilage to obtain the Bar Professional Training Course at a chambers just behind the Temple.

Please understand that there is considerable competition for such pupilages. It took me a whole year of applications before I was accepted. I had to complete my advocacy training course and practice management course in that year. I was called to the bar after successfully completing my Bar Professional Training Course and the requisite number of qualifying sessions. Despite all of the dedication and sacrifices I was still not offered an immediate tenancy, but did an additional six months squatting at chambers, after which time I became a tenant.

Like most barristers I was self-employed, and it took me well over a decade before I could even contemplate that I had achieved a modicum of success. For many years I barely made enough money to pay my rent and board. Indeed in the current times, there are many criminal barristers who take cases where the fees do not even cover the travel expenses to the court, but take the case due to the constant pressure in chambers to remain active. A barrister without a reputable portfolio will not survive long in the current profession.

By the time I was put forward as a Puisne Judge by the Office of the Lord Chief Justice, I had already spent a quarter of a century pursuing my legal career.

There were many occasions that I contemplated seeking another course, particularly early on when I was so unsuccessful in gaining a pupilage. But I retained a level of self-conviction, which undoubtedly came from the support of a strong, resilient family that helped me through these times of self-doubt.

Ultimately it is the morality - or lack of it - that is common place in the lives of many of the defendants that stand before me who are involved in such serious criminal offences, as the one that you are interested. The greatest influence on morality is the boundaries set by the parents or guardians during the early years of a young person's life. I have spent a lifetime dedicated to the legal profession and the administration of justice, but I am not naïve or blinkered to the fact that the bedrock of justice is the moral boundaries established in the family setting.

I can say with absolute surety that if it hadn't been for my wife and parents, I may not have had the strength to complete my training. In those early years, when I was struggling to be called to the bar, and prior to be recognised as a worthy barrister, my wife, Marian was my rock and my staff.

Marian has been my staunchest critic and my most avid supporter. We were married just after my graduation and moved into a tiny flat in Fulham. She was a policy advisor in the Heath government, working in the Ministry for Health and Social Services under Keith Joseph. During those early years she was our main bread winner, working long hours, maintaining our home comforts and tolerating my self-inflicted depressions when the smallest of my cases didn't go well. Her self-sacrifice and loyalty deserve the greatest accolades.

She gave up her career to bring up our children and help provide the stable home environment that has allowed me to pursue my ambitions. She has brought up three beautiful children, all of whom have achieved their own successful paths in life and of whom I am immensely proud. Her energy has never diminished. At times she is busier than me, undertaking charity work in our village. She has established a network of close friends; a network that regularly meet and of whom I never tire.

Indeed, a young person's moral compass is defined by the boundaries set at home and reinforced by the law, not the other way around. My morality was ingrained at an early stage and reinforced by my wife. Doing what is right by my family and knowing my family gives me the strength of conviction to strive and achieve. Marian and I have been together for over forty years, and I would say unequivocally that time has never diminished my affections for her.

These four young men that stood before me in this case all came from homes where little effort was put in to define right from wrong. I could see no evidence of a stable father figure who could guide them. Indeed, on reflection, I cannot recall any case such as this where a father figure features. A sad indictment on our society, I am sure you will agree.

No, I make no excuses for my family life, or my upbringing. However, it does appear to me that whilst government focusses its efforts in strengthening the legal framework to address gang associated violence, it would be wiser to turn its attention to addressing the social malaise that creates an environment where morality can so easily be sacrificed for financial or personal gain. It is indeed a sobering thought that a person's moral compass can be so easily diverted by the value of a small amount of monetary gain or a personal disagreement, ultimately resulting in the taking of a life, over a dispute which could be resolved through debate and dialogue.

I am sorry but I really have to draw this to an end. I hope you have found it useful and if you do need clarification on any of the points that we have discussed, I am sure my clerk would be more than happy to assist. Let me show you out

Chapter 18
Samuel's Story

You want me to tell you my story? Then you need to understand who you are talking to.

I am Samuel Ojafutu.

You get me?

I am Samuel Ojafutu.

I am Sizer. I'm no wannabe street gangsta. You need to respect who I am, you understand?

I said someone should write a book about me, people can learn a lot from my life. I've got real experiences that no research will ever tell you. Man, I am research.

I am Sizer.

My father was an army officer in Gambia. He was part of the military coup, led by Lieutenant Jammeh who overthrew the corrupt President Jawara. My first memory was lying in a tent with my two brothers, waking up to the sounds of gun fire and people screaming. It was brutal. I saw this man dragged out of his tent, pushed onto his knees and shot in the back of his head. You could see part of his brains splattered in the dirt. Yeah, it was brutal. His body lay in the dirt for hours and we just stepped over him until a truck came round and took him away.

We left when I was 5. My mother took me and my brothers out in a truck with lots of other women and children. We were travelling for what felt like a lifetime, following the roads across Senegal, all the way to Tangier and then by boat into Spain. We spent 12 months in Germany and then came across through the Netherlands and by boat to England. I don't remember much 'bout the journey, but it took a long time and we slept in the back of trucks or a container. I was always hungry. That's what I remember. I was always hungry.

My dad didn't come with us. He was an army officer so he had to stay and see out his duty. I was 9 the next time I saw him. We were living in our two bed flat in Sandby House on the Glebe Estate, off Peckham Road. Tunde, my older brother, was 11 and just started secondary school at St Michael's.

My father wasn't a brutal man, he was just a disciplinarian. Man, failure wasn't an option for him. He would beat us if we did wrong, if we didn't keep our room neat, our clothes folded, or didn't clean the dishes right. He would beat us if we didn't clean his shoes right or were late for dinner. He taught us there is nothing wrong with discipline; you step outta line, you get punished. He beat me and my brothers more than my mum. He was hardest on Tunde 'cos he was older. When he beat mum, he would tell us why he was gonna do it. He prepared himself. He told us what she had done wrong and then he would strip to the waist, take off his belt and beat her. On one occasion he got Tunde to do the beating to show he was a man. When he finished she had to say sorry to all of us.

He told us that a man and a woman must know their place. You get what I'm sayin'? He was teaching us respect. There is a hierarchy, lines that can't be crossed, without punishment.

He told us about his time in the army, what it was like being an officer; the corruption in the government. He taught us how governments were built on lies and corruption and the only way that man can survive is to fight every day. You only got to look at the government to know it's true, with all their sleaze and scandals. People in government are just milking the system, screwing us over. Man, we're not the criminals we're just finding ways to survive while the MP's take us for everything we got.

We moved from Sandby House when I was 10. It was just my brothers and my mum. My dad had been arrested. We spent 9 months in a shit hole bed and breakfast off the Queens Road. The room was 10 foot by 12 and we shared a bathroom and a kitchen. Then we got a flat on the Friary Estate. It was 2002 and, man, it was mad. There was loads of shit going on. Damilola Taylor had been dead nearly two years and there were media looking for any gang story. One time a film crew offered me and my bros £20 if we did some gang poses. Back in the day it was mad.

To start with we got a rough time on the Friary. You gotta understand that back then if you were from other ends, you were in deep. We had to take steps to protect ourselves. Best way was to get a street rep; getting a name meant getting accepted, so we went out and proved ourselves.

By the time I went to secondary school, my brother had already made a name for himself. He was hard, stabbed someone with a scalpel during a fight on the school ball court area. He was dealin' at the age of 14 and got sent out to Ipswich and Norwich to deliver and pick up. There was two years difference between Tunde and me and three years between me and Ismail. But we were very different people. Tunde was hard but dumb; olders exploited him. He was their muscle. At 16 he was 6 foot 5, intimidating and hurting people. He had learnt his trade from our father who knew that the fear of violence would demand respect.

Ismail was much quieter and had brains. Ismail had the protection of our rep, you get me? So he used his intelligence wisely. We had Ismail working on getting money out of some of the small time dealers, the ones that didn't have protection. It was just a little tax, that's all. Ismail would link with them and say they should pay him a small percentage. Course everyone said no. So Tunde and I went to see them. After that they paid Ismail. We gave half our cut to the olders. That's the way it is. Everyone has their place and we had a reputation to build, we were going places.

Me, I had charisma. Everyone said so. My teachers said I had charisma. I played them, using my charm. There was this one teacher, she was fresh, but straight up she was so naive. Tunde and I talked about staying after school and banging her in the class room. I could tell she wanted it, she was so tight.

Yeah, I had charisma and them girls couldn't get enough of me. Whenever I was out with my bros it was always me that the girls moved on. Timi hated it. Man, it got right under his skin. He thought he was so smart but I had the whole package - looks, money and rep. I never had to move on dem bitches, they were on heat. I'd throw them some line and they were hooked. I was 13 when I first had sex with a girl. She was older, 14 or 15, I think. She was one of Tunde's girls. She was round with him and said I was cute. We did it on mum's bed.

No one could touch me. None of my bros could even get close. Living on the Friary there were names who were watchin' me. I got close with one of them.

Tut, no I'm not giving you his name, you dumb or something?

He took me places, linked with bros from north endz. We did parties on the coast. We always did some business. I was moving shooters by the age of 15. I had drivers that took me around, they knew their place and if we ever got stopped they took the rap. Yeah, you wanna write a book about a real gangsta from back in the day, I am the man.

I had my heroes, people who were like me, that demanded respect. When I was 13 or 14 it was the Babeboni brothers. There was Timi who was a hardened killer, having witnessed his father being butchered to death back in Sierra Leone. His younger brother was Diamond, but he was ruthless; even the olders feared Diamond. They stormed a christening on the Woodene, guns blazing and robbed the whole congregation. Shot some woman dead. Man, they were fearless gangstas.

Back then, Peckham was the place. Everyone feared us, even the crews from Brixton. We would go and storm an estate in their endz, or a club and cut it up, but they were scared of reprisals.

My bros were close back then, but you know the truth is they were street punks. They all looked to me to make things happen. Anton was a nobody. He never had the bottle, man he was chicken, always leechin' off me and KJ. Michael thought he was a rapper, going places, but he knew shit. I could spit better than him.

No, man, I had it all. I've still got it all. No one messin' with me in here, you get me. You mess with me and I put it on you, watch your family suffer, no word of a lie. When Tunde was 16 and I was 14, this girl turned up at our house, shooting off her mouth about wot we did to her brother. We spliced his face or bust his jaw over some money he owed, I don't recall which. But she stood screaming at us, that she would do this and that. Timi went after her with a machete, dragged her back into the house and we raped her; even got Ismail on her. We took photos and sent them via BB, it was mad, that broadcast was going viral. That shut that bitch up. Police came round and arrested us but she knew what would happen if she opened her mouth and chat shit.

Man, Peckham was ours, we ran the streets. The olders ran us. But they let us loose. We gave them the profit and kept business tight. We ran lines out to the hicks, Chelmsford, Cardiff, down to the West Country. We had boys out on errands day and night. No one could touch us.

When I was 15, I came back to the house early one afternoon. I knew something bad had gone down the moment I walked in. I went up to mum's room. She was lying on the bed covered in blood. Her face was battered, her cheek bone was caved in. There was this cable wrapped round her neck, it was a cable from the bedside lamp; looked like she'd been dragged by it. Her arm was all busted up and at a wrong angle. I went into the bathroom. My dad was hanging. There was a rope up through the loft hatch.

I went next door and got a neighbour to call the police. I was calm, but I didn't wanna talk to the fedz. Mum survived. I don't know how, but she survived. Truth man, I never thought she was that strong. But she suffered hard at the hands of that man and she must have got it into her head to see him out.

She was in hospital a whole month. Me, Ismail and Tunde made a pact to stay low when she came out. Don't get me wrong we kept our endz tight but we cooled the beef. You understand? We had boys out doing the business, but out of respect for mum, we stayed off the front line.

Of all my bros KJ was closest. KJ was straight, you get me. He was on point. There was just black and white with him. We got an errand, we delivered. Someone messed up, they paid. Anton wanted a rep but never wanted to earn the stripes. He was just a wannabe. He was never one of my crew. But Timi wanted him 'round. Reckon Timi just wanted some boys who he could twist to do his thing. KJ reckoned it was Timi that got him shot; set KJ up with some youngers who he was enlisting.

See Timi always saw himself as a big man. He hung round the olders, always working away using his intellect to set an inside line. But KJ and I saw through him, we knew he wanted a position so he could take over our endz and run the business. Reckon he got the shooter from Andre and set up some boys who wanted their own rep. They weren't up for it and messed the hit. See Timi never got it. You wanna take someone out you gotta do it yourself. But he never wanted to get his hands dirty. He always thought he was too good for that.

I called Timi's name you know? It was after a party and there was this bitch there that he and Anton were sweating over. She was just playing them. So I turns up, man she was all over me with her eyes. Timi started some stupidness but it was a party, I was there to chill, get some pussy, but Timi just wanted to mix it up. Like I said, Timi never got his hands dirty, just used others to start the beef. Got me and Anton at each other, over some shit, but he got me mad. So when Anton faced me out I was all ready to bust someone up. Man, Anton was so stupid, listening to that low life, but he was even more stupid facing me out. That's the thing that my dad taught me, you gotta earn respect and then you gotta keep respect. Facing me out in a party was dumb. I was going to bust his head wide open until he was dragged out.

When Timi heard I'd called his name, he ran scared, you understand. He was so out of his depth, I had him dangling. We didn't see him for weeks, holed up under the skirts of the olders, like the coward he was.

I want you to write this down so that you get this. I don't hate my dad. You might wanna write some psychological shit that my dad was abusive, so me and Tunde became violent. I know what you are like, tryin' to moralise, about "people are a product of their upbringing." I've heard it all. The shrinks in here talk about it, even that stupid judge started off that madness. You tell me what some old fuck like a judge gonna know about my life and my background. No, I want you to get this down. My dad was strict. He believed in discipline. He didn't beat us all the time and he gave us respect when we earned respect. If he beat us he told us why. It wasn't random. You understand? But we never went short of food. He taught us the importance of earning respect and keeping respect. You get me? It's the earning of respect that counts and then maintaining it. You let another man take that respect away then you are nothing. You even worse than if you never earned it in the first place.

KJ, now he never went out his way to earn respect. KJ never expected nothing. He was marking time. Don't matter what he did, he never saw it as good or bad. For KJ life was for surviving not living. No one could force KJ to do anything, you could never get him to change road. But he was straight and I respected him for that.

No word of a lie, I was there when Anton got shot. I knew shit was going down, you think I'm stupid or something. Me and KJ knew there was beef and that we were being named. Decided to take the initiative, take the higher ground.

Had this hunting knife, I called it "li'l sizer." Funny huh? We set things up. Even wrapped Timi in to make amends. Yeah, I would have shanked Anton, stop him shooting off his mouth. But the rest you gonna have to work out yourself.

Fedz wanted someone to pin it on they were always gonna come for me and KJ. We didn't expect anything different. No one in Peckham was gonna snitch on us. The word got out and it really wound the fedz up. But Darell shot his mouth. Man that nigger forgot whose side he was on. He's a dead man walking. My boys are gonna track him down and bust him open.

Wot! You asking what I think of the fedz? Man you really are dumb aren't you? The police are the biggest gangstas on the front line. Those that aren't taking bribes are fucking over the ones that are! You must be really stupid if you don't know that. They even worse than the government! There's this copper who's related to one of the GAS gang. You wanna know why they never got turned over? He fed them the lines.

Back in the day we bought off more fedz than youngers. How you think we ran the endz? (Tut) You really are dumb if you think that the fedz are clean! Even them Trident officers are screwing each other over. That's why no one ever snitch to Trident. They just turn you over and bang you up, no word of a lie. This older made a big mistake of feeding them when they said they would give him protection. Next they just cut him loose, some of the olders got hold of him in Streatham and sliced him up in broad daylight, in the middle of the afternoon.

You cross one of your Bredrin, you pay it off, you snitch to the fedz, you're a dead man, even if it takes a lifetime to track you down.

I've got boys chasing Darell down. They have their orders. Man, he will suffer. Yeah, I still run the streets from in here. My boys know the score. My appeal is in 6 months, reckon at worst I'll be out in 5. Then I'm gonna bust it up. Had a reader in and the spirits are good. Yeah I'll be out in 5. First thing I'm gonna do is rape Timi's girls, every one of them. No one's gonna touch Timi 'til I come out, but I'm gonna make sure people give him a message - there's no rings gonna protect that piece of shit. Selling out all of us for his own ends. Man, he's gonna get hit hard, he won't know what's happened.

Yeah, I saw Anton's mum. She kept writing to me pleading me to see her. She asked me why I killed him. Man you know what, I don't rightly know. Man was just in the wrong place at the wrong time.

Yeah, you write that story about me. You tell it how it really is. I am Samuel Ojafutu; I am Sizer. I am the real deal, none of that wannabe shit. You ask about Sizer, you look at the fear in the faces of those on the front line. I'm not part of a story, man, I AM the story!

Chapter 19
B's Story

You know I like my rep. Yeah, I like it. Took me 20 years in an' out of jail to work out what real rep feels like; 20 years of losing everything I had, pretending I was the big man, gettin' moved on by the police and then back inside. I lost count how many times I done time. Last time was 3 years for handling - 3 years!

Yeah, I lost everything. That's what I tell the boys I work with, you know. Wasn't until I became a mentor that I realise that people respect me 'cos I can turn people's lives around and inspire people. You know, I get genuine gratitude.

You wanna know my life? Rah, that's one long story. You know, why don't I tell you my life like I tell the boys I work with? I worked with Andre. I worked with Samuel. I worked with KJ. I worked with Michael. You know I worked with every one of them, but you gotta know that you have to treat them as individuals. Rah, your life is your life. I've seen men beaten inside, 'cos they think they got protection. I learnt some hard lessons over the years, but the hardest is that you on your own. No one comes visit you when you lost everything and inside; no one. Not one of your crew, just family. And it's hard seeing your family hurting 'cos of the pain you caused them.

So I treat these boys as individuals. That way I get them to recognise who they are, not some false big man, street rep.

Let me start with Andre. See, Andre is like me. You know, I look at Andre and I see me, through stages of my life. See, my mum was a drug addict. She and my dad came over from Jamaica; she was from Hanover and he was from Kingston. I'm the youngest of 5; my mum and dad had another son who they left in Jamaica. I didn't know about him 'til I was in my teens.

Life was hard. When we came over we lived in Tottenham, just off West Green Road. We got washed in a tin bath. We didn't have much food and when I went to school I got bullied 'cos my clothes didn't fit or I smelt. My mum and dad split up not long after we arrived. Mum got a boyfriend and she would pack us off to Dads to get us out the way. Then she took an overdose. You know we were in an' out of care all the time from when I was 5 or 6. We got split up; sometimes it was good, sometimes it wasn't, but eventually we would all end up back with mum.

So when Andre told me what his life was like as a boy, I got it. I understood what he meant when he said life was hard and he had to fight for what he could get. I was Andre, you know; I was in his shoes. Mum was a drug addict and financially things were hard. I went to West Green Primary School. I remember wearing two pairs of socks 'cos the soles of my shoes were worn out. I remember sitting in assembly refusing to cross my legs 'cos I didn't want everyone to see my feet were bleedin' through the holes in my shoes.

The humiliation - it runs deep. I never felt like I fitted in, never felt like I had the right clothes. You wear what you were given basically, you understand?

So yeah, I got it with Andre. He had to establish a place in life and so did I. We talked a lot about his life and mine. We both used violence. Neither of us started out that way, but by the age of 8 or 9 we both knew that we weren't gonna get the breaks other kids got. Suppose in our heads we knew we were on our own, you know? I'd tried getting kids to like me. I used to go to the sweet shop across the road on my way to school and knock stuff over; sweets and stuff. I used to just give them out at school. Never asked for money, just wanted some friends. But the moment the sweets ran out the kids just moved off.

As I got older I grew big, you know. I didn't really get into trouble but I started to get a bit defiant, you know, giving attitude. I saw how people reacted - teachers and pupils. I could see they were wary. I didn't do anything about it though, not at primary school. I just started to think I had some control of my life. Being the tough man gave me a place, more than tryin' to buy friends.

I went to Stationers school in Hornsey when I was 11, now Park View. There was this white family lived across the road. And this little skinny white kid, his mum said to me to look after him. I was big and he was skinny and I suppose she thought I could protect him, you know.

Anyway these boys from a proper criminal family started picking on him. We were in the playground and they surrounded. So I watched them for a bit until I saw this kid get pushed down by this bigger kid, so I moved on him. We had a big punch up, but it got broken up by the teachers. So you know, he wasn't having it; suppose he had the rep of his criminal family on his shoulders so he told me it wasn't over and it would be on after school.

I'd never been in a proper fight you know. But there I am after school surrounded by all these kids? And I'm thinking, boy I'm in deep now! So I rushed him. Suppose he wasn't ready, but I caught him, one punch, BAM! He was gone.

So it's started. He got olders from the upper school to bring me down. Next day I'm going at it with one of them. This time the punch thing wasn't happening and we're wrestling and tryin' to take chunks from each other. Now I've grabbed him round the neck, but I'm clinging on cos' I'm getting' tired. Then just as I let him go he passes out! Boy, I'm telling you, I thought he was dead, so I just run.

They suspended me for three days. I was angry you know 'cos it wasn't my fault. The system just punished me 'cos I was standing up for me and my friend. But government's got a way for punishing those that's hurtin' the most.

But you know, nothing was as bad as the beatin' I got by my mum. Boy I'm tellin' you that was the worst beatin' anyone ever given me.

See, my life and Andre's goes deep, you know. It's not that we didn't have people we loved - we did - but we also carried pain from early. Andre loved his mum and his brother Kelvin, but he was too young to protect them. I loved my mum but she just seemed to push me away; she couldn't cope. I didn't realise it at the time, I just saw it as rejection, you know, she never got my pain from feelin' I wasn't wanted. Andre worked at St Gile's and we would talk lots about life and prison. I was in an' out of secure units and prison from 15. We talked about running the wings, how we used to run our little scams and hustle. I was into double bubble, selling weed, sweets, biscuits, hustling phones. We used to rip up bed sheets and weight them with hair bushes so we could swing them from one cell to another to pass gear. You know, I was the best at hustling. Everyone came to me, "B you got this, B you get me that."

Then the screws would come in and bust my cell and take my gear and it would start again.

1984 to 2009 - looking back I can see everything. 1984 to 2009, from age 17 to 44. All those years I hustled the streets, or I hustled the wings. You know what I got to show for it? Nothing, I didn't have a penny to my own, just regret. My mum grew old and sick and I didn't have nothing that I could comfort her with. Rah, you gotta lay it bare. I was a loser; a has-been gangster who had bought into a dream that was never gonna become a reality.

You know, I saw it all in Andre, man. He was so close to getting out, you know. But that one last time when he should have gone silent, he didn't. Sometimes road runs so deep you can't see the truck before it hits you. I saw Andre in prison, few weeks back. I feel for him, you know. He knows he's lost everything, but he's too scared to admit it. Man, I feel for him.

Now Samuel, he was another piece entirely. How do I describe Samuel? So, back in the day, the hood was full of little punks like Samuel. Rah, you can tell who's the real deal and who is a street punk. Shooting his mouth off about this shit, or that shit; Samuel was just like all the other street punks I crossed.

You know, there was this guy in my class at Stationers, thought he was some big shot. He starts calling me nigger this, nigger that, you know, starts all this racist shit. So we're changing classes in the corridor, and I'm thinking, "I'm not gonna take any of this shit," so I grabbed him, threw him on the floor, stood on his ankle and leg and said to him to apologise. I'm a lot bigger by then - 11 or 12 - and I've grown. So I'm holding him down by standing on his leg and I'm bouncing on him, to make him say sorry. Next thing I heard this crack. Man I was so scared I ran to my class. Next thing, I get hauled up in front of the head master. So I tell him what the boy called me and he says if I apologise then that's the end of it. But I ain't apologising - the boy called me a nigger, what I got to say sorry for? So I got permanently excluded. But I'd sooner get excluded than apologise to some punk who should be apologising to me.

When I was older, about 18 or 19 I ended up in the adult wing of Ashford Prison. I'd been in and out of juvenile units since I was 14 or 15, but I kept on doing snatches and burglaries, then escalated to some harder stuff. Anyway, we hit a jewellers up West somewhere; grabbed a whole lot of trays, so all these police turn up on Broadwater Farm looking for us. But back then it ran deep with the police and us. So, people are coming out of their houses and it starts getting hot. That's when you know you got real status, when whole families are coming out to cover your back.

Anyway, cut a long story short, I end up in Ashford. First thing you learn in adult prison is make a mark. You don't make a mark you gonna get beaten. So, you know, I was popular 'cos I got visits, got weed brought in and did my hustling thing. Anyway there is this punk who keeps asking for weed, so I give him some. You know this guy tries to mug me off; I gave him some weed and every time I ask him for payment he's making excuses. I'm working on the hot plates and every day I'm saying you better pay me and he keeps giving me this sarcastic smile. It's getting to the point that people are looking and wondering why I'm letting this punk disrespect me. I'm feeling like an idiot now; worse I can feel my rep sliding. Like I said, you let your rep slide on the wing, you gonna get beaten.

So anyway, Saturday's recreation day; we do this run and then we get to play football. So we've been playing football and there's the guy in the changing room after the match, sitting on the bench getting changed. He sees me and I say, "You got my money?" Like I know he hears me 'cos he looks, but then just ignores me and carries on with his little crew. Now I'm riled you know; he's seen me and totally disrespected me, right in front of everyone. So I walk very slowly over to where he's sitting and as I get up to him, BAM! I kick him with the flat of my foot straight into his face. As his head comes down I bring my knee up, BAM!

Anyway, he's lying there in this pool of blood and his face is shattered, blood gushing out. I was literally so scared I was confessing; ended up in D1, segregation for 5 months. I was told I'd be on murder charges. Man I was scared, real scared. Life! I mean I never even thought that they could do that to me. Like when you're in prison you get used to punishments for misdemeanours like not making your bed, petty stuff. You get used to shake downs and running your little scams. But life! Man that hit hard. I thought:

"B, this is it man, you messed up big time. Your life is over!"

Any road, this guy was in hospital for 4 months 'cos they had to reconstruct his whole face, you know. When he came out he got released. They said that he had served his time. So the charges got dropped. Man I'm telling you, someone was looking down on me that day.

I wanna tell you all this 'cos there is a difference between names and street punks. Names like me and the crew from the "Farm", we weren't violent people; we never went out of our way to hurt people. We did robberies and snatches. We did spotting, watching people take large amounts of cash from a bank and robbing them. We used to buy mission cars for a few hundred and sell them on a week later, but we never used violence. We were in it for the money, not hurting people. But you crossed us, you call our names, then we would use violence. Like I said, when you on road or in prison, you gotta protect your rep at all costs.

But Samuel never got that 'cos he was just a street punk. Rah, violence should be a means to the end, you know. But Samuel thought that violence was the starting point.

I tried to get him to understand that bullying and threatening and intimidating people didn't make him a man. I even tried to use the example of his dad and the army to get him to understand that it is not the use of force that wins the war, it's how you control your force; use it tactically, when and where, that leads you to victory. You know, over the years since I turned my life around I realise that violence is really a display of weakness. Violence is just the inability to control your emotions. You get more out of life if you channel your emotions and turn them into positive energy, you understand me?

No, Samuel never got it. He kept telling himself that he was the big man day after day, until finally he totally fell for his own lie. He ran errands for the olders thinking he was protected, when all they were doing was using him. His only rep came from what his brother had earned. When he was off road, Samuel became a mule, but 'cos he believed in his own hype, he never saw it. I told him what would happen, if he kept playing the big man that he would be set up. I've seen it time after time, but it wasn't what Samuel wanted to hear, so he shut it out. Rah, it was only time before he got set up. Now he's in prison he's gonna learn some hard lessons. I had a visit booked recently but it got cancelled 'cos he'd taken a beating and was in the hospital wing. That boy better start learning fast I'm telling you.

Michael, well, Michael was the opposite of Samuel. Michael was a quiet boy. He was musical and had real talent. I met him one day at the studio on Walworth Road. He'd been there two days and he played me some of his music. It was deep you know. It was rap but not gangsta rap; it was about life and his journey, like where he was. Rah, it was dark, I'm telling you. It took me right back to when I was a kid and some of my memories. I'm telling you, it brought a tear to my eye.

See, when I was a kid I really just wanted people to understand me. No, sorry, that's a lie. I wanted my mum to see me. I thought she never saw me as a person, as her son. Like I said, I was the youngest of five and we didn't have much. I got that, you know. But what I didn't get was that the thing my mum had least of, was time for me.

I was in and out of care and then when I was in my teenage years, I was in out of secure units. Somehow or another, I always managed to break out. I remember when I was 14 I ended up in Stamford House in West London. It was an assessment centre with a secure unit. My mum and the social worker took me and I remember thinking it was another care unit. When I got there, they took me into a room and then a holding cell. They took all of my clothes and put me in this uniform. I refused to wear it and sat in a cell for hours refusing to put it on, until I was so cold and hungry I just gave in. I remember sitting in that cell, screaming for my mum to come and get me out. But she never did. Reckon she was already on the tube back home.

I was at Stamford House for about a month or 6 weeks before I broke out. I worked out that if you had toothache they took you outside to the dentist. So I ran a scam and the moment I got out I made a run for it. Of course, I went straight back home, you know. So, I'm at home and mum makes me some food and next minute, there's a knock on the door and there's social services.

So, now I'm back in the secure unit at Stamford House. So I play it cool for a bit, play the system. Then I worked out that the education unit is right next to the path where the visitors come in an' out. So I sign up for some wood work class. There are prefects, like trusted inmates that take you between the blocks. So this prefect is escorting me down to education when, BAM! I'm gone; down the path and out the gate.

Next thing, I'm back in Stoke Newington. This time I don't go home right away. I nick some stuff out of the shops on Green Lanes - clothes and things - then I head for the Shabines; play some music, smoke some weed, have a little party. Shabines are like chill out joints, could be the back of the shop or a front room in a house. You pay a bit of money to get in or, if you know them, they just let you through.

So, I'm there a few days. But after a while I get homesick, so of course I go home, you know. Guess what? This time it's police at my door!

See, every time I got sent away I would always find my way back home. I got sent to Stamford House, out to Arnold's Lodge in Grays, Essex, even a boarding school down in Dorset. Every time I broke out, did some crime to get food and clothes, hang around the Shabines, but always end up at home. See, despite all of the hardship I still loved my mum and I just wanted to be in her vision to see she loved me. That's what Michaels music took me back to; being a teenager, feeling lost and not knowing how to tell her that I just wanted her love. I still carry that feelin' you know. After all of these years I can still feel it inside me; wanting to be seen and for my mum to hear how I feel. You don't always need words to know how someone feels.

Michael got that. Of all of those boys I worked with I liked Michael the most. He was quiet, not easy to get close to, but when you did he would open up about his music, girls, all that shit. He wasn't academic like I know his friend Timi was. He didn't do great in his GCSE's, but he was bright you know. He had some great plans on runnin' his own business, but I don't think he ever quite believed in himself enough to make them real.

It took me a long time to work out why Michael was linked with Samuel and KJ and the other boys. I couldn't understand it at first. He had a mum and a dad. They both seemed to really love Michael and were concerned about him, particularly after he got stabbed. They had a nice house, not on an estate and they worked real hard to keep things going. You know, that's one of the issues. Lots of the parents I work with care about their children, but they workin' day and night just to keep things going. Michael's mum and dad worked long days, I'm tellin' you. They out from early and not back till 8 or 9 in the evening. Michael is an only child and I reckon being on his own was tough. Having some friends to hang meant a lot to him.

But that wasn't the real reason Michael got linked with these boys. Looking back on it, it's real clear. It was the boys that wanted to link with Michael more than him wanting to link with them. See Michael was real important. He had the talent. His music was gettin' a lot of hits on YouTube. SB-TV was onto him and producers were lining up to work alongside him. See for the crew, Michael could do music that hit the masses. His influence could reach more people that their street corner crew and get them the rep and influence they wanted. So they worked on him, real hard, made him the front man, you know, the face and voice of their crew. Man, Michael couldn't walk the streets without being stopped. We went north side once, took him to my ends just to chill. I'm telling you we got stopped walking through Bruce Grove, like he was some superstar.

It all changed for Michael when he got battered. Things got hot one afternoon on the front line. A cafe owner - who was a known older - got attacked. Anyway, I reckon Michael was there. He was walking home when he got attacked and hit with a baseball bat; fractured his skull real bad. If it wasn't for one of his friends calling an ambulance, I don't reckon he would have made it.

After that Michael stopped doing the music. He refused to do anything that put him in front of the public. He stopped engaging with me and when he finally did I couldn't get anything from him. I know he stayed close to some of his friends like Timi and Anton, but he cut all of his other ties. He was never on the streets and last I heard he was working with his dad.

I reckon the whole incident with Anton started from that night. The streets were so hot after that and it never really died down. When you've run the streets you know the signs; less people out, more drive-bys. You start seeing some of the names in places you never seen them. Then there was this big barbecue party when it kicked off. That was the spark, but the fuel was all ready to ignite from that night on the front line.

So the last one I worked with was KJ. Rah, man, KJ was deep man. Not deep like Michael, no; KJ was emotional deep. KJ carried a hurt so deep I reckon it cut into his soul. I never really got to find out what he was carrying, he never opened up as much as that, but I recognised it. I felt it even if I didn't get to the root cause, you know.

I remember the day that I really decided to go on road - I was 14, nearly 15. It was half term. I had been in the boarding school in Dorset for a few months. It was one of those places that was ok. I got a little respect from the head master. He even took me and a couple of others shopping on Saturday and bought me a little radio. I'd never had a radio before and it was my prized possession. I used to draw up the bed covers at night 'n' listen to the channels. It was like being in a world of my own.

Anyway, it was half term and I'd been lookin' forward to going home, being with mum and the family and some home cookin'. Back home, space was tight and me and my brother shared a room together. So picture this, yeah, I get home and go up into my room and there's only one bed - my brother's bed. So I went downstairs and said,

"Mum where's my bed?"

She didn't have an answer. So I says,

"Rah, you guys never planned for me to come back home!"

So she gets all defensive; my brothers are tryin' to calm things down, but I ain't havin it. I'm real riled, so I take my radio and I smash it against the wall and storm out.

Rah, I can feel the anger beatin' up on me right now just talking about it. That's the moment I start shutting down. I'm arguing all the time, picking a fight when there's no fight to have. But what I'm feeling most is that I'm not belonging. Do you hear me? That's the moment I knew I didn't belong nowhere and to no one. It's a painful feelin' when you realise that there's nothin' in life for you. It's like the whole world is moving around you but there is nothing for you to hold on to. Everything is revolving but it's revolving without you, like you don't exist.

That's it. That's how it was for nearly 30 years. And that's what I saw in KJ. There was nothing going on in his world that touched him. He'd shut down, just like I had shut down. The sad thing was, I couldn't reach him back then. But there was one more experience we shared that I didn't realise until recently when I did a prison visit.

I must have been in my mid-thirties right. I was in Pentonville. I'd done some serious shit by then and been into the whole gang thing - couriering, serious robberies and living it up. I was dealing and using; weed, cocaine, the works. So I'm in Pentonville, just reflecting. For the first time, I'd shut myself up; didn't get involved in the whole running the wing shit. I was just reflecting that I was gonna lose my flat that I'd worked on and I was getting these feelings of hopelessness about what I've been through. I was having a reality check, you know what I mean? I realised that I got nothing to show for the years of criminality, and the truth was the authorities just seen me as someone who likes prison. I was becoming a great pretender.

Rah, whilst I'm going through all this I get a call - my sister's died. I'd not seen my sister for years. I'd been inside prison for so many years that I'd missed the whole of her life. And now it was too late. So I get taken to the funeral in handcuffs. I looked at all my family, my mum and my brothers and I felt ashamed.

A few weeks later, my mum had a stroke. They took me to see her in hospital 'cos she was so bad. When I saw her I was shocked, really shocked. One side of her face was all distorted and she couldn't speak. My brother said,

"Look mum, B's here!"

She tried to say something but I didn't understand. It broke my heart. Rah, I'd wasted all my life and lost everything I ever had. Worst of all, I'd lost all the time I could have had with my family and I knew I could never get it back.

That's what I could see in KJ. KJ was no gangster. He was lost and had lost. Saddest of all, he doesn't know how to find himself. His mum died a few months back whilst he was in prison. I know he went to the funeral 'cos I went. KJ just stood on his own; he looked lost. I knew that look and it touched me deep.

No, prison is no place for KJ. Prison has it place, you know, it can get some people to get a perspective; might get Samuel to realise that he has no real rep. None of his crew ever gonna visit him in prison. But prison is no place for KJ. KJ is already in his own prison and there's nothing gonna touch him being locked up.

Rah, I've learnt some hard lessons over the years. When you are caught up on all the gangsta lifestyle there is always someone else who you are in contention with. You're always thinking,

"If my name isn't ringing I'm a has-been."

People are saying,

"Who are you?"

But truth is you aren't living in the real world, it's the gangsta world that is the fantasy. Then something that really touches you happens and you wake up and realise you lost everything that was important.

When I work with these boys I want them to understand that their past is, or was, a journey. Life is all about change. You don't have to let what you have done define you, you know, you can be defined by your future.

You know, I can use my story, everything I lost, to make them realise that the street is a gambler and everyone knows gamblers always lose! I lost a lot. I can't get any of that back but being a mentor has regained my self-respect. See, when I work with these boys that I mentor I can see where they are coming from. I can use my skills, that I have developed through life, to challenge their thinking and thought process, you know. I can challenge them about why they make certain decisions? Are they really their decisions? I can see it 'cos I lived it. Every one of them has strengths and I can help find them, encouraging them to capitalise on them make them see a win-win situation with education or training or employment. Yeah, I get them to see a path to respecting yourself. That worth more than all the money you can earn as a G.

Like I said, I like my rep now. It's based on genuine respect, 'cos I'm helping people. For the first time I got respect from my mum. When she looks at me she sees the real B. I thought I would never see that and it means the world to me. She doesn't have to say anything; I just see it in her eyes.

Chapter 20
Jade's story

Listen, I don't want your sympathy.

My experiences have given me a self-conviction and a strength that I would never have had without them. I knew all the boys on the front line. It wasn't like I was forced to be friends with them and do the things I did. A lot of it I'm not proud of but I'm stronger for it. I know my strengths and can deal with my shortcomings. You make life work for you, take the knocks and move on.

I want you to understand what happened to me so I'm going to start by telling you why I ended up on the streets, living the gangsta lifestyle, running with all the boys - Andre, Chimer, Li'l Z, Raz, Reefer, yeah all of them on the front line. I was born in Croydon, and lived there all my life.

There was me and my mum and my brother and sister. But I remember from early feeling like I'd lost something. Like, despite all this family there was something wrong with me; like a piece was missing. Yeah, like I was a jigsaw and someone had lost the last piece.

See, my brother and sister knew their dad. Their dads would come over or take them out. I was the only one who didn't know their dad. Like, I knew who my dad was, but he was never a father, you get me. He never came to my school, I never went to his house; he was absent from my life. So I felt more rejected. When I was out shopping with my mum

I used to look at the faces of all of the men around me and think,

"Could he be a dad to me?" because he looked into my eyes or:

"Is the guy my mum was chatting with someone to be my dad?" because they looked close.

When I was at primary school I used to get bullied which made me feel even more alone. I never told my mum. She had enough to deal with and I used to think,

"If my dad cared he would protect me."

But just thinking it made me feel even more rejected.

My mum was single for about 5 years. We all used to think she was lonely so we kept on to her about getting a boyfriend. So when I was about 11, going on 12 she met someone. He acted like he came with the right intentions; got real friendly with us all so everyone liked him. The whole "not having a dad thing" was going on, so I got fooled real easily by him. We were sitting together one afternoon when he started touching me and making comments. I was eleven. I can't describe how I felt 'cos it hurts too much just thinking about it. He said if I ever told anyone he would get his gun 'n' friends and come and get me. I believed him. He had this way of always being in places that we were on our own. He would put his hands on my thigh and then under my skirt, inside my underwear. I could feel him inside me. I was so scared I just froze. Every time he touched me it felt like he was robbing me, do you get me? Like he was taking something precious from me that I would never get back. I still feel that way just talking about it. That's why I'm crying. He robbed me like I didn't mean anything. I was just 11 and he violated me and robbed me of my dignity and it took me years to understand what he did to my soul.

So, I started staying out to try and keep away from him. First I'd hang around the parks and ride buses. Then I hooked up with some of my cousins from Peckham. It was a legit excuse to stay out and one that gave me some cover from all the questioning. By the end of year 7, when I was 12, I was already on road, rolling with some of the boys. I would go to school, sign off the register and then go off. Yeah, I hit the streets hard because the abuse at home was ten times worse than any abuse I got on the streets.

It wasn't like I didn't tell anyone what was going on at home. I told the deputy head at school and he called mum in but she didn't come. They took me to Mayday hospital to check me out. My hymen had been damaged but was still intact.

I felt like the whole world had let me down. I didn't feel brave in telling people. I thought people should have seen what was going on. I'd gone from being a shy, bullied girl, to being in a girl gang in the space of less than a year and yet no one saw it for what it was. Worse of all, I felt angry. I was angry with my mum and my brothers. My brothers thought I was sleeping with all these olders that I was hanging with, calling me a "hoe", when the real truth was I was running from the house 'cos that man was abusing me.

What you gotta understand is that there was no "home" for me. There were no warm loving parents and sympathetic siblings who saw me for who I was. No one bought me clothes and gear. I didn't have food to eat until I got the money for it. I didn't even have any sanitary towels unless I bought them. It got to the stage where my family were more relieved when I was out, rather than concerned that I wasn't home because by then I was just seen as troublesome. Looking back I know my mum loved me. She's proved in a million times over. But she didn't know how to deal with me. We've talked about it, so many times, but back then I was hurting so much that I couldn't see anyone else's emotions. I couldn't see that she cared, even though she did, cos I could only see my pain, my hurt. You get me?

There was a part of the North Peckham Estate we had been told not to go to, particularly as I was from Croydon. It was seen as entering into enemy ends and we would get beaten and raped if we went there; but I was fearless back then, what had I got to lose anyway? So I linked with some boys I knew who I would go and smoke cigarettes and chill around Bradfield's Boys' Club with. I had one school friend from Peckham side called Rochelle, so I hooked up with her and started mixing with her crew. I just thought it was better to change my life than own up to the truth about why I was hurting. I couldn't cope with the stigma of people knowing, so I adapted my life.

Even then from the age of 12, I had learnt the art of hiding what hurts you most. Looking back, most of the kids that I hung with from Peckham were hiding. Rochelle had been raped by her father; Tyrone's mum was a crack addict; Kevin had lost both parents to terminal illness; and Steph had been offered to older men from the age of 6 or 7. She tried committing suicide on at least two occasions that I know of. Chimer was beaten by his father. He suffered real bad at the hands of that man. There's a lot been said about Chimer, that he was the enforcer for the olders, but I know a different Chimer. We would chill, smoke some weed and he would tell me stories about what happened to him. The abuse that he got from the age of 2 shocked me. Can you imagine what it must have been like to have been whipped, locked into a trunk for hours or to have cigarettes stubbed out on you? He learnt not to cry because he knew if he cried he would get beaten even more. Chimer told me he wanted out, to move away from the gangsta lifestyle from early. It's not that he didn't know how to do it; he just never had an alternative lifestyle as a back-up plan. He knew violence, that's all.

I could relate to Rochelle and Chimer, Reefer and the rest. I fitted right in. I had a group of people that I could relate to and who never asked any important questions. I started smoking and doing shake downs on other girls just robbing them of everything they had - money, phone, jewellery; back of buses, then on the street, McDonalds, wherever we could get away with it. The jewellery was usually trash but it was the fact that I could take it that was the thrill. I felt guilty afterwards. Especially this one time on a train when this girl was begging me not to take her ring; it was her grandma's and it was all she had left of hers. She was crying and everything and it made me feel sick doing it but I took it all the same. I couldn't lose face in front of the crew; after all I was getting a rep, the one that set the pace. I kept the ring in my room for a while, but it sent me crazy, so I threw it away. No, I'm not proud of what I did, but even back then I had started to live by the rules of the road and I was in no position to turn back.

We hit any place that we could get money, particularly places where there would be no comeback. When we had no money on a Friday we would go to this youth charity. Some of the older boys would kick off big time, start facing up to staff or threatening the youngers. The boss woman would come down and pull the boys into her office, give them £100, sometimes more. We would get the money and go and cash up, buy weed or smokes, booze, then moved on to buying typhoon bikes which were the craze. Sometimes we would meet up at the charity down in Camberwell and get food or even clothes. It was such a breeze that we just got everything we could, no questions asked.

Then I got nicked. I was 15, on a robbery and extortion charge. Seems that they traced me through a phone. I thought at the time that I must have just got careless and used a number for too long. But, man, I was tired. I'd literally been living the streets for over a year. No one cared for me; no one asked if I was ok. If I didn't rob I didn't eat. So when I got nicked I just thought,

"If I go to prison I am a real G and, after all, what's harder that being on the streets?"

I was on remand for a while. Then I went to court at Woolwich and got sentenced. I ended up in a secure unit in Rainsbrook for 13 months before getting moved to Rochester.

On the streets I never thought about family. All I thought was that my family let me down. On the streets you have a unit and loyalty but you don't have to love. Street gives you the time to stop thinking. Inside your bed is warm, you have friends and you have food. You start reflecting; you miss your loved ones. Mum came. My little sister came as well. She said she dreamt about me being home and then woke up and I wasn't there. After a while I asked them not to come. It's easier doing the time without seeing people you care about.

I was in Rainsbrook and Rochester for a total of 2 years. None of them was hard. Like I said, nothing's harder than living on the streets. I kept linked with my unit. I was still telephone ordering from Stamford Lodge, organising for when I got out. I never got messed with inside. See, my mum's family are Campbell's. The Campbell name carries weight, many of my uncles and cousins have built up a reputation and on the streets and in prison that means something. So the Campbell name carried rep inside, plus I had a unit outside that were making a name. Anyone who thought about messing with me knew I had the names to hurt their family outside through my family or my unit. Just one call, that's all, to a cousin or one of my crew. I call you name your family gonna get hurt.

When I got released I was banned from Peckham. I could "reside" in Croydon. What a joke. Of course I still went back. Back then I saw Peckham as my endz. My unit is all there. They were my family.

Of course it was never really about Peckham. I could have linked anywhere and it would have been the same - Brixton, Hackney, New Cross, wherever. I'd entered into a gangsta lifestyle because I couldn't emotionally deal with what happened to me. So I started to develop a persona on the streets that gave me a sense of belonging, you know. I trained myself to be someone who I wasn't, so I could be strong and survive without the need for anyone.

So, when I came out, I started to earn my own money, run my business that I had set up from inside. I knew enough road men, so I bought some weed. Back in the day, I paid £120 for an ounce and broke it down to draws or eighths or 20's. Depending on how you split it you can get 17 or 18 draws to the ounce. So by the time I'd paid the man back I would have £40 - £60 clear. How did I get the £120? I robbed of course. A few of us like Li'l-Z and Samuel's older brother, Tunde, did some till scams to get the first payment.

The boys I would hang with on the front line gave me respect as well - Andre, Reefer, Chimer, Raz, all the old names, I hung with them. I was younger by 3 or 4 years, but we were close and they never gave me a hard time. They had all served time like me, so they had a prison mentality about them. I started dressing like them, not in colours, that was for the youngers, like Samuel, who were always jarring around us. No, we wore Averex and Loony Tunes, real expensive stuff that made us stand out. I would have been 17 going on 18. I cut my hair real short and bought a moped so that I could get round to deals more easily. I never had any licence or tax, at the time I wasn't bothered, it was all about street rep and earning money. By then I was turning over £300 a day. I had smart clothes; I paid the basics and started filing my room with gear. I bought expensive make up, got a fridge for my own food, had a phone installed. The road men taught me that the sign of success was the amount of stuff that you had, so rather than buying one pair of shoes or one nail polish, I would buy three or four to show I had money.

I would go to all-nighters with my friends, get drunk, chill or go to clubs. My brothers tried to clamp me down by locking me out or even locking me in, but they wasn't wise enough and I always worked scams around them. Like I said, home held no place for me. It was just a place full of pain and suffering and I just viewed the restrictions as an unnecessary inconvenience.

All that money that I went through, I must have wasted thousands. None of it changed how I felt, though; I was still lonely. I did my thing to hide how I felt inside, to make up for the fact that I felt disfigured, cheap and dirty. By this time I had got it in my head that the best way I could get back what I had lost was to take everything I could from people to punish them for what had been taken away from me. But looking back now, it was that I actually wanted to be noticed. I wanted to punish, because the people who I thought were there to protect me didn't see the hurt I was suffering. They didn't see it or they chose to turn a blind eye to it. So not only did I feel violated, abandoned and unloved, I also felt it had to be my fault. After all, my dad had chosen not to know me, my mum hadn't loved me and my brothers thought I was a hoe. Yeah, punishing people got me noticed, and I was someone you had to take notice of.

Looking back on it, I was really messed up. When I was a bit older I got a copy of some of my pre-sentence reports and I read them through. There was this one incident that stood out. It said that I had gone to the back of the bus to rob some girls. There was one girl eating some chips, so I grabbed them and started throwing them at her and shouting;

"Hey you fat girl. Fat girl like you doesn't need no chips."

It said that the girl was scared and started crying so I slapped her across the face and then got off the bus. I'm reading this report and I'm like watching this scene in my head, of me at 13 and this girl. I felt so ashamed that I was once that person.

Boyfriends? I had one serious boyfriend; started when I was 13, before I went inside. He was one of Reefer's friends. He would have been 17 or so. I suppose I was looking for love and I had it in my head that if I get with a gangsta I would be quite hood. As I had nowhere to stay I moved in with him. I lost my virginity to him, but he had real anger problems. He used to get violent with me, threaten me if I did the wrong thing or was chatting to a particular guy. I remember once he dragged me up, boxed my face and forced me to strip. I was begging him,

"No, please don't do this to me!"

I was terrified of what he was going to do, but once I was naked, he just sat there staring at me with this manic look on his face for what felt like ages. I was too scared to move. Then he said,

"I'm joking with you."

After I came out of prison I got back with him. He begged me from early, saying he had changed and didn't realise just how much he loved me. Although I had my unit and had my scams lined up to be a road G, my self-esteem was still real low. Remember, I didn't have any proper relationship to call on; I was still just a little kid inside. So I got back with him. I didn't move back in with him. By then, mum had got some sense about her boyfriend and lost him from her life. She wanted to try real hard with me, so she had done up my room and she let me have friends stay. But she wanted me stay in. Suppose she thought that me being in was better than running scams with my unit. But I was 17, no just turned 18, and staying in was hard. I'd worked hard inside to maintain my business and keep tight with my unit. So I was running a double life, one to save face with my mum and one as a roadside G. It was hard 'cos I knew both were lies and I began to question what my life was all about.

Anyway, I'd been out three months - I had just turned 18. It was Christmas and we were having this big party at my aunts. All my cousins were there and it was a proper Campbell family gathering. By then I knew there was something going on with my boyfriend. I had an inkling that he was sleeping with my best friend, so I ran a test. I telephoned her with a message about my boyfriend. Within a few minutes he rang me, so I knew he was with her. So I rang her back and faced her out. She didn't have an answer to my questions, so I told her what would happen to her if he ever called me again. You can only get hurt so many times when you become immune to the pain.

Most of the boys I hung with treated me like one of them. Remember by the time I was 15 I had a bigger rep than some of them. Add to the mix that I was a Campbell. They knew that messing with me meant messing with the Campbell family, and my cousins had their own notoriety. Some of the youngers tried it on - Samuel and Timi - but they were youngers. They were jarring all the time and I had no patience for them.

What! Samuel said what! That boy's lucky he's inside or I would bust his head open right on the spot. No, I never had sex with Samuel. I wouldn't ruin my rep on a piece of low life shit like that. See, Samuel is like all of those street runners. They get a bit of cred and they think they've made it. He was always mouthing off about how big he was and he had protection. I can tell you straight, Chimer had him marked, used him to run some business and was about to set him up. Boys like Samuel were two a penny, no brains and no connections. He was always going to end up in jail or dead.

Don't get me wrong, there were lots of girls on the scene. They would come sniffing around looking to get a little street rep of their own by hanging with a name. Some did it for their own interests - getting gifts and taken to all-nighters. Some would do it because they were just stupid enough to fall for the wrong guy. Their big mistake was ever thinking that these guys were ever going to be monogamous. The olders used me to square off things with their "gilts" whilst they were off doing their business with another woman. I would lie to them, go round and chill with them to keep them busy; I wrote out Valentine's cards or bought birthday presents. It was insane, but back then it was about protecting the boys, because for me, they were my unit.

There were some girls who linked up for other reasons. My friend Rochelle for example, she would link up with any of the boys who showed interest, sometimes two, three at a time. She was good looking enough to have her pick, but like I said, she had her own problems that she was carrying around. She had an abortion when she was 14. Some said it was Reefer's but I know different. She told me she fell pregnant after her dad raped her, like he'd been raping her since she was 6. No, Rochelle had a lot to deal with. She didn't care about who she was with, but then she got a rep for being a cheap girl so the boys would just use her and pass her around. It was painful to watch.

There was one of the olders that I got close with, after I finished with my boyfriend - Andre. Andre ticked all the right boxes. He was light skinned, so my gran liked him. He was polite and his family was from the Islands, even if they weren't from the right ends of the Islands. He was older but that didn't matter and it didn't matter that he was a road man. That was never going to be an issue with my family as long as he was respectful and didn't take liberties. Andre and I got real close, but it was never going to work for us. We knew too much about each other, how things worked, the scams and the deals. Emotionally, we were poles apart. Andre wanted me around for protection and I wanted him around to feel protected. There was never going to be a middle ground.

Andre got arrested and jailed. No word of a lie, he got lined up by one of the olders who cut a deal with the police. They were waiting for him coming out of his flat with a kilo of food and 5 g's. He knew the score. Our relationship came to a sharp end. I had no use for a man inside and he had no use for a girl on the streets. Andre was back out after 2 or so years but by then our worlds had moved on.

It was big lesson for me, a real wake up call. I had a choice and I knew it from that day, so I started to explore routes out; real ways that I could become legitimate. I got into Croydon College and started studying business management. I carried that area, working in McDonald's to start with. I was only there for a while when I had to quit. All my unit and the boys kept coming in expecting free burgers and the manager faced me out. I got a job in a fashion shop on; their clothes were all very bootleg. Then I got a job behind a desk, can't quite remember where, but I hated it. I wasn't even 17 and I wasn't ready for being sitting behind a desk. After that I was offered a job in a travel agent in New Cross. The guy said he'd pay me £500 a month, but he was longing me out, like a power walk. So after three months I quit. He paid me some of my money when Reefer and Raz went round.

I didn't tell the boys that I was going legit straight off but we talked about it. I kept my links because I needed them around. I still kept some business going because I still needed the money.

One of the hardest things about coming off road is the money; going from up to 3g's a week to a few hundred isn't easy, particularly when you have to keep up a street rep and carry on paying the olders. You can't walk away if you are in debt and you can't walk away if there are scores unsettled. So you have to slide out by keeping the people that have influence really close and making sure they know you have other, legitimate interests. Remember I was involved with olders. I was only slightly older than Timi and Anton, but since I was 12 or 13 I had hung out with the olders. So the people that held influences in my circle were Chimer and Reefer.

Everyone wants to get out you know. None of the boys want to be a road man forever. So if you move to get out and become legitimate and you don't double cross anyone, you can do it. But you have to do it slowly and take one hurdle at a time. The front line is a place where everyone is paranoid of everyone else. You seen with the wrong person, or have beef with a member of the crew then you can suddenly find that the whole of Peckham is on you. So you have to take the opportunities that life presents, use them to start a different life, as a different person. That's what I did. So I started work and then my course. I got settled and talked it through with the boys.

My real change started to happen around Christmas when I was 19. I'd been kinda legit for a while - had a good job, my own car - but I was still close to road men. I was still carrying a lot and I was hitting life hard. I would work long hours all week, sometimes until 8 in the evening and Saturdays, and then I would party all weekend. I spent my money on clothes and jewellery and make up and would never go out unless I was wearing all the gear - hair done, false eyelashes, the whole works. I was hitting the weed hard, drinking, the works. But the pain was still there. You do things that give you a sense of numbness. Hitting life hard was my way. But there was nothing I did that could hide the pain forever.

One Monday morning, after a weekend of partying hard, I had an altercation with a traffic warden. I was going to get the car because I was late for work when I caught him giving me a ticket. I begged him to let me off of it, but he wasn't having none of it. I don't remember exactly what happened next but I just lost it, went crazy. The police turned up and had to restrain me. I spent two days in a cell after that and went straight to Court where I got 2 months in custody. The fedz looked happy. They notified my work, so when I came out I lost my job.

That's when I tried to take my life… Can we move on?

So it's Christmas and my friend says to me,

"Why don't you come to Christmas Mass with me?"

I didn't want to go because we were heading to a party, so she says,

"Come on just come with me. We will go to the party after."

I'm not happy about it but I can see it means a lot to her so we go and I'm sitting at the back and the priest starts talking about suffering and that God can see our suffering, that he can see our sins and is willing to forgive us. He said that God can look into our heart and help us with our suffering. And it was like he was talking straight at me, and I'm sitting there just crying. I'd promised myself I wouldn't cry, but I'm sitting there, crying.

I can't stop thinking about what the priest said so, the week after I go back, and I keep going back week after week. To start with I just sat there listening to the words, soaking up the energy. Don't get the wrong idea, I didn't suddenly turn to God, it wasn't some kind of vision thing - what do they call it - an epiphany! It was nothing like that. It was that I began to feel like I belonged. Like, I wasn't being judged, more that I was being accepted. Every week I went back made me feel more and more that this was a place that I belonged.

My church is Greater Grace Ministries. I've been going ever since that Christmas. I am part of a family!

Huh? Haha, yes I suppose it is like my unit, but we focus our energy towards different ends! I'd never thought of it that way. Let me write that down so I remember!

I do believe in God? Yes. God has given me a spiritual strength and brought me to a different place where I can understand my life and where I want to go. It doesn't mean I have to accept what happened to me, but I have a belief that God has a purpose for me and I can use my experiences to help others who face the same challenges. I have been blessed with a vision that can see behind the image that others on the road portray and help them recognise that they have real choices, not limited ones that the road men offer.

I carried on running some business on the side for a while to keep sweet with the olders, like covering things with their girls. But bit by bit I eased away. After a year I had stopped running lines, I handed the business over to Reefer and he split it with some of the road men - Samuel and Timi.

That's where all their beef came from. Samuel was always a road man, but Timi, well, Timi was something very different. Timi was way too smart to be on the road. He always had a big plan to go to university and be involved in big business. So he used the front line as a way of cutting his teeth. He was the ultimate manipulator and he did it in such a way that everyone got sucked in by his intellectual persona. He must have had influence because he was well protected.

Samuel reckoned he was the big man on the road, but Timi was working behind the scenes to undermine him and take away his line without him even knowing it. He was going to use Anton to do it, but he didn't realise at the time that Anton never really had the bottle. So he set Anton and Samuel against each other.

Yeah, I really liked Anton. He and I hung together. I was too frightened to get real close to him but we definitely got on. By then I was already beginning to work on my getting out plan, so the last thing I needed was someone like Anton jarring me. So I pushed him back. I suppose in another life Anton and me would have hit it off. But there was no room for me to be linked with someone like Anton, a boy from the front line, when that was the life I was trying to move from.

I don't know what happened that night on the block. Truth is I don't want to know and I don't wanna talk about it. See, seeing death changes you and I had enough of knowing a part of me dies every time I hear of a death. All you are left is the memories but it's the memories that bring the pain into reality, your lost, I can't describe the hurt, its too deep, that's why I cant talk about it.

You think someone could have stopped it? But you can only say that from your perspective, not from the view of someone who's spent their whole life on road.

There is one code. Loyalty. Deaths comes by that being broken.

Yeah, Anton was different.

I can't make it up. But that was the moment I really cut my associations. My big change was giving birth to my little boy 6 months later. When I pushed him out it was like pushing out all of the badness, all of the animosity and hatred that I had built up. My world totally changed. I could focus all of my energy into this tiny little thing that was totally dependent on me. I could make up for all the things that had happened to me and I vowed to make sure that he wouldn't face the same indignation that I had suffered.

I finished my night school and got qualified. Now I'm working in the City. My relationship with Mum has transformed and we really get on. I can kinda see where she was back then, when all this started. We've talked a lot about what happened and I kinda understand now that there are aspects of your life that make you blind to other things. I would be lying if I said I've recovered from it. But when I joined the church I realised that you can't ask for forgiveness if you aren't willing to forgive. Being willing to forgive helps you heal.

Brandon is 3 now and I've made sure the boundaries are set from day one. I don't take him to nurseries in Camberwell or Peckham, I take him to Dulwich. When we go to play clubs or go out we go to Bromley or Sutton, same with shopping.

I still live in Croydon, but my relationship with the boys in Peckham is different. I feel safe linking with them, but that doesn't mean I have to associate with them. I don't rely on Peckham, but for the first time I can recognise an affinity with Peckham. When Brandon, gets to 8 or 9 we'll move out, make sure he's in a good school with good prospects.

When I look around, all those on the front line from back in the day have moved on. Andre's in prison, so is Reefer.

Chimer is dead. That was one of the worst nights of my life.

I'd not seen him for months. I'd been busy with work and my son. But he linked me and started begging me to go to a nightclub with him, so I went. There were all of the old crew, but it was relaxed, no beef, just chill. Chimer is cracking jokes and making us all laugh. I've never seen him so loose. The next minute shots are being fired and the place is in pandemonium. Everyone was running from the club and screaming. I stayed with Chimer until the paramedics came. I'd been involved with road guys for over ten years but I'd never been close to death, yet there I was sitting next to my friend Chimer watching him die. Life takes on a different meaning when you are close to death.

Rochelle, she's got two kids. She moves about, working the lines every now and again, holding straps. She's on the game when she needs money, which is most of the time because she's taking smack. Looks like the family history keeps repeating itself.

Who is Brandon's father? I've no reason to say. Frankly I don't want to discuss it. I don't need his type of help. I don't need his road man money or his protection. He's my child. I want him to have an active relationship with his dad, so I promote it and allow access. But he is my world. This is my journey now and I won't let anyone get in the way. I have my family, my brother and sister, my mum, the Campbell clan. And I can trust that God will show me the right path for him. He is my inspiration and I want him to know we will always have a bond that will never be broken.

I've got a life now, my life and there is no way I'm going to allow anyone to get in the way and destroy it. Brandon will grow up knowing his own mind and have his own self-conviction and self-determination. I won't let anyone take that away. I know that God is there to support me and guide me through. My son and my church have given me the strength to survive and that's what I'm going to do. I can't hide from the past, from what happened to me and what

I've learnt is that all that gangsta road thing is just a way of hiding. When I look in the mirror now, with all the make-up stripped away I see me, not someone hiding behind a roadster image. I see me, a young woman in control of my life, blessed for what I have, knowing the past can't hurt me anymore.

Regrets? Yes. I have real life regrets from my days on road. It hurts. It hurts because it makes me feel vulnerable, because my past can still come back and take away what I have, what is important to me, what I have worked so hard to make good. When I lie in bed and start thinking, listening to my son's quiet breathing, I think of his innocence how his life will be growing up. I want to protect him, keep him safe from my past.

Yes, I have regrets. But this is my story and I will use it to make a difference, do you get me? This is personal. I can't stand by and watch the same cycle going on, watching more people die on the streets, knowing that some family will get a knock on their door, tellin' them that their son or daughter is dead. So yes I have regrets on what has happened to me, on what I have done. But I gonna channel my experiences, use my faith to break the chain of violence. That's real, that my life.

So, you gonna help me?

Chapter 21
Respect and Reputation

So we come to the last of the 5 dynamic factors that define gang violence, the one most talked about but so little understood - respect and reputation.

Respect and reputation can come in a number of guises.

Jade had the reputation of a whole criminal family with its own, self-perpetuating street rep, surrounding her like a protective bubble. She may not have recognised it during her early years on road, but it was there, subconsciously acknowledged by the olders that she called her unit. Being part of a large extended family with criminal connections, provides a level of security that cannot be emulated by many of the boys on the front line. Growing up, her unit were more reliant on her that she gives credit for. None of the olders got too close to her emotionally, none of them tried to take advantage of her, sexually abuse her or rape her because they knew the reputation of the Campbell family. Such acts of disrespect are tantamount to signing your own death warrant and that of your family.

Andre did not get set up by the boys on the front line. He actually got set up by olders, another family, because someone in Andre's family had crossed them, a cousin, or brother or a distant relative. How they had crossed them, where and when, is long before Anton's murder. It was an old score, probably drug related, but a score which had gone unresolved. But these incidents do not remain unsettled. Unsettled, and the likelihood is that it would be seen as a sign of family weakness, bringing no end of wannabe boys to their door, challenging them. So they set Andre up. Let Andre get complacent. Saw the opportunity with Anton's murder and took it.

The reputation of a family with a name is held in high esteem. For those on the front line, these family names have a more powerful influence than Saatchi and Saatchi, or the Kennedys, Goldsmith or Murdoch. The influence of known families like the Campbells is far more tangible, far more real, and far more likely to wreak revenge over personal conflicts or disrespect. They may not have the same institutional power as a 'Ford', but they can have you shanked, your brother kidnapped or girl raped. That's real, that's personal.

Bringing shame on the family is just as bad as trying to shame a family member. You do not cross those lines. Timi liked Jade, but his first instinct was to use her name and his association with her to buy himself greater influence. But he was smart and the realisation of what it meant being a boyfriend of a Campbell quickly sunk in. Anton however was more emotional, more attuned to his senses. He did not see the pitfalls because he genuinely liked Jade. All of his friends recounted that. The demise of Anton was because Samuel saw this compassion as a weakness and exploited it.

Similarly, the reputation of a sibling, cousin, father or uncle who was involved in gang violence provides a street status. Unlike the family who for generations has been steeped in lucrative criminal activity, the reputation of a sibling who has already worked their ways through the ranks means that you, the younger member, have to maintain that status. You will be tested from a young age, even as young as 7 or 8. You will be required to hold your ends, dish out punishment and protect your name at any cost.

There are families where the second, third and fourth brother have had to reinforce a reputation, often resulting in the ultimate personal sacrifice. Because the world keeps evolving and recreating new scenarios on the front line, the next family member has to raise the stakes, go one stage higher, in order to define their own warped identity.

But unlike the established families, there is little protection beneath the reputation of the older sibling. In fact you are - as the next in line - more vulnerable than if your relation had never been involved in the first place. You are an easy target. Taking out a younger with a sibling rep can get you noticed. You might end up being protected, groomed by an older, who will give you their street name, "Tiny Andre" or "Li'l Chimer", to give you an immediate status or 'rep'. Protection is everything; your longevity on the road depends on it. But you still have a shelf life. You are still expendable, because there are plenty of others who want to take your place, only they are cheaper, more malleable and a little bit more depraved than you are.

When your brother is dead, or your cousin is in prison, the protection of your family stands for nothing. There is no safety net.

For young women, respect and reputation comes in an abundance of shades and colours. Some young women use gang association to gain respect, by having a boyfriend with a street rep. Some want to be in a gang because it gives them the personal reputation of a gangster, allowing them to rob, threaten, intimidate and inflict violence on others, to demonstrate their dominance. Some want their own reputation because life is shit at home and status on the street gives them belonging. That was Jade's motivation.

It's not a popular conversation, but it would be wrong to apply our 'middle England' stereotypical understanding of the natural vulnerability of being a young female and place it in the context of how that vulnerability is exacerbated by being in a gang. Young women who associate with roadmen do not look at it that way. The gang offers opportunities that have not and are unlikely to be offered to them, in any walk of life that they have, so far, experienced. Those opportunities can be emotional or material; sometimes they are cathartic, personally cleansing, a way of shedding years of pain and suffering.

It is not the vulnerability of being a young woman involved in a gang that is the issue. It is the vulnerability that they already carry and which is then exposed by being part of the gang that is the issue.

Vulnerability is the fertile ground where gangs can sow the seed of belonging, nurture it until belonging becomes belonged and then exploit it for their own ends. Gang members of both sexes are arch manipulators, identifying each other's emotional weaknesses and exploiting them. After all, they will have endured similar experiences which brought them to the front line in the first place. That is their emotional connection, however subliminal it is.

So, unlike the boys, the issue of respect is defined for young women by the reputation they gain whilst they are associated to the gang, which in turn defines what their route out of the gang looks like. For Rochelle and Marline, they are baby mothers. They will always have an umbilical tie to their men which they can never break. It will always come back to them. As the reputation of their man dwindles, his emotional dependency will increase, for some turning to anger and violence, for others a place of sanctuary which they can rely on and abuse, perhaps as one of many similar baby mothers in different areas, even different towns and cities.

Yet for KJ's sisters they are immune to this. They never got involved and they shunned involvement. They were older and took the opportunities that life presented them and moved on, up and out. Perversely it was KJ's lack of protection from having no predetermined reputation that helped. They were never going to be drawn in because KJ had nothing to lose. The respect that he had was self-gained. There was no status earned by an older sibling, there was no older to protect him. KJ built a reputation by placing value on nothing, including himself. Interestingly, those young men who are the most chaotic, most violent and psychopathic in their actions, so often have the same emotional void as KJ. Watch them shed any attachments and dependencies, give away any money earned and disown any friendships that have developed, to create a perfect storm of emotional detachment that allows them to take a life or inflict pain without a moment's hesitation. Do others respect them? No. But their fear is fathomless.

If you go to the English dictionary and look up the word "respect", it will be defined as, "admiration, to value, to revere, show consideration for". To have respect for a person is to have a high regard for. That was the motivation for the surgeon and the police officer. They had strong positive roles models in their lives which helped shape their direction and gave them the personal motivation to achieve.

On the front line, however, "respect" is not a positive thing. It is not something that you can be proud of, nor is it something that you have earned though positive, righteous deeds. Respect on the street is built by fear, by proving how strong you are, that you can and will hurt anyone for anything, however big or small. Respect is about punishment, intimidation and violence and as a result it is built in shallow, unstable ground, where the foundations can crumble the moment a stronger more violent breed steps in to take your reputation away.

Compounding this is the world of social media with its fast moving variety of mediums, providing the opportunity to promote yourself and challenge others. YouTube clips can be made and uploaded in less than an hour; Facebook allows you to self publicise the characteristics that you want people to buy into; Snapchat allows you to create your alter ego; and Instagram lets you publish those images of you that shows how popular you are, or should be, to others. Our young generation does not draw a distinction between the online social media world of virtual relationships and the real world. They see no difference. It is an easy migration which opens up endless possibilities of interactions across areas and cultures.

For gangs and gang members it is an instantly accessible opportunity for self- promotion, to reinforce your image and reputation, challenge other gangs, challenge others or display your access to guns. Gang raps of violence and threats against others are part of that alter ego, specifically used to display the sophistication of high quality musical talent, with raw, disturbing, extremes of violence. Reality and alter ego combine. Social media plays one of the biggest parts in the building of a reputation and reinforcing a status to such an extent that not being able to access the social media world is like being permanently thrown out of your group of friends.

So to preserve respect, to keep your "rep", you have to continue to prove yourself, punish hard and show no weakness, use every medium real and virtual to promote yourself and "dis" others. Anton was right to fear KJ over the £20 bag of weed that he lost. KJ knew the rules of the front line and the only thing he had to lose was his rep. Nothing else mattered because he genuinely did not care about anything or anyone. I will never forget sitting in his kitchen, the day before Anton's death and trying to persuade him to look at other paths in life. But for KJ, there was never another path because he never valued his life.

You see the ultimate learning is that status and respect might mean everything on the road, but fundamentally you cannot change anyone involved in gang violence, if they do not respect themselves. If you do not value yourself; intrinsically recognise some deep rooted self-respect, then you cannot place a value on anyone or anything else. So hurt and pain is easy to inflict because you feel no hurt and pain. You became immune to such feelings, when you saw your dad butchered, or mum raped, when you were raped by a member of your family or step father, or saw your sick brother die of a chronic disease that you are powerless to stop, when you watched your mum die or when the one person you relied on was taken away. Emotional detachment numbs the pain but does nothing to heal the wound.

So running drugs and hurting others earns a status and by violently enforcing that status you earn respect, and by robustly maintaining respect you have a reputation. But, as Jade said, the one thing you never have - through this journey of earning money, by any means necessary, to build a reputation, to make up for the emotional trauma of life - is trust in anyone else. Trust no one, rely on nobody, watch your back and keep your own counsel. Andre and KJ, Timi, even B, will tell you that you soon learn from jail who your real friends are on the road, because you never get visits in jail, other than from your closest family.

That is a lesson that Samuel still has not understood yet, but he has got years inside for it to really sink in. And whilst he might think he still has a hold on the streets from his cell, those people who have been doing his bidding have only done it for their own ulterior motives; to gain status, earn money, get a rep. The world on the front line turns fast. The salient lesson is that the front line is not reliant on anyone; it is self-perpetuating, sucking people in, spitting them out, moving on.

The hardest part of the any new journey in your life is the very first step, whether it is changing your job, moving housing, beginning or ending a relationship or starting a family. However, it is impossible to take that step if you do not respect yourself, do not value who you are and recognise the value that a new journey in your life will bring you. Fundamentally, our starting point for understanding the respect and reputation by which we define those on the front line is not in terms of their impression on others, but by the respect they have for themselves.

This is the crux of the issue. If we want to make a difference to the urban gang violence, our starting point should be redefining "respect". The conversation should not be about the reputation of your family, or your brother, the status you have from protection of named olders, or the notoriety that you have from elaborated deeds, the alter ego you create through social media or even the respect you demand of others because of your rep on the road.

The starting point of the conversation should be about self-respect; how do you value yourself? It is the most important question to ask those involved in gang violence, but it is the question we ask the least.

Silent Voices

Fully understanding the respect you have in yourself is the first step to coming "off road". From that point on, nothing is impossible.

Chapter 22
The Killer's Story Part 2

Anton was being set up. I knew it 'cos Timi told me. Timi and I were close, he was a good friend to me and Anton, even when Samuel was calling Anton's name, Timi stood by us.

I got the gun from Marlon. He had connections through his dad. I told him what was going down so he helped get the gun. I'd never held a gun before. It was much heavier than I thought it would be.

He gave it to me with 4 rounds; that's all he could get, 4 rounds. I thought I could scare Samuel by showing him the gun and firing off a round. Let him know that we had connections.

Then Timi BB'd me to say things were going down. When I got to the estate I saw Anton going in to the block. I called to him but he kept going, so I ran inside. I went to the lift lobby, but the lifts weren't working. I was panicking. I ran up the stairs and heard voices. I tried to pull the gun out of my waist band and it snagged. I wrenched it free as I opened the lobby door and it just seemed to go off. I heard it go off in my hand. It was so dark and I didn't know what had happened.

I was so scared.

I just ran out as fast as I could.

Silent Voices

I didn't know that I had shot Anton. I never meant to shoot him. When they told me he was in hospital I wanted to die. I never meant to hurt him. I just wanted to protect him.

I loved him.

Please understand. I loved him.

He was my brother.

Epilogue

So did anything actually change following Anton's murder? Did his death act as a catalyst in the lives or the direction of any of the characters in this story?

After all the characters are real. However hard it is to comprehend, each one of them is real and the stories told are real, even if the facts and locations are altered. These are people who you might pass in the street, stand next to in a bar, and even work alongside. They are not distant individuals who are from another universe; they live in the flats you see on your bus journey, crossing the road or as you are stopped at a red light.

Timi is at university having won a scholarship. He wants to be a lawyer. The murder of his friend had a profound effect on him and he draws on his experience to try and change the judicial system; a struggle he will continue with into his professional life.

Samuel's appeal failed. He is beginning to realise that his status on the street is gone and keeping his head down in jail is his safest option.

The teacher is married. She and Alex have a little boy and are living back in Cambridge, close to her family and all of their support.

The judge remains as insightful as ever, but is pressing the court's administration to create opportunities which allows him and his fellow judges, to understand the pressures that communities face in places like Peckham.

Having recognised the battle he was facing in his operating room the surgeon is delivering education programmes on knife crime in schools, desperately trying to get students to understand the true risks of carrying a weapon.

The police officer is 18 months from retirement. He is not looking forward to it. He will only be 52, but he has had enough. All the changes in the Met had made him disillusioned. He knows they do not want people like him, close to retirement and steeped in the culture of the force. So the lack of respect he feels in the force correlates with the lack of trust from the community during the investigation into Anton's death. Although he would love to give this case one last crack, the workload and his closeness to retirement means it will never happen.

Jade, however, is flying. She has been working in recruitment for over two years and she is doing well. She goes church every Sunday, praying to God to help her to find peace with herself. She has stopped hiding herself behind all the bling and make-up and people are seeing her for what she is, a beautiful woman who cares about others and wants to protect them from the ordeal she suffered. She is doing talks in schools and setting up her own community project to help single mums get into employment. She still carries an emotional fragility with her, ingrained by the years she had of having to hold her suffering alone. But she is willing to share it more with others knowing now that by exposing her inner feelings it will help her heal. But she cannot let go of the control of her son, who is as strong minded and independent as her mother - they will have some real rebellious battles ahead.

I would like to tell you that everything worked out for KJ and Darrell. I would like to tell you that, in their own way, they moved on with their lives, found a skill they were good at and some solace with someone who cared for them. I am afraid I cannot. I do not know if it will work out for either of them because they have not even opened that chapter on their lives. I worry for them both all the time. I saw Darell last week and he was having a good day. He has his own place now and is going to college in the autumn. Let us hope he sees it through and those dark days do not envelope him where he gives up hope on himself and his future.

KJ has become even more introverted. His psychologist relays his concerns and writes asking his sister to visit, but her life is busy and full of all the pressures that we create that makes our days fly by. KJ does not have those luxuries; time remains the one asset he has plenty of and is the one thing he needs least.

There will be more to tell of Darrell and KJ, but not now. Their stories are far from defined and for the moment you will have to make your own conclusions depending on whether you are an optimist or realist.

Marline has disappeared. Andre knows. He is a broken man.

And Anton's mum, what has happened to Anton's mum? Her simple humility has touched the lives of hundreds of young people as she goes around and talks to them about her boy and the loss she has faced. She tells them of the beauty of life and the joy of seeing your child born and grow up proud and strong. She touches hearts and makes people weep as she describes her pain and the pain of Anton's brother, of the best friend that he has lost.

She is changing people's lives, she is making a difference, she is touching hearts and saving souls. Anton's life and his death has meant something and it has made a difference. But some nights she cries herself to sleep. Some days she does not have the strength to get up. Birthdays are dark days and the anniversary of that fatal day is still full of sorrow and grieving. A day never goes by when she does not think of her beautiful boy and she still misses him.

Anton's death made a difference. There are many young people, now adults, who remember him for good reasons and still hold him as an inspiration. Speaking to one of them recently he told me that he changed his life from the road because of Anton. He wants to make Anton proud.

And what of the author?

Government cuts took away his job. A necessary efficiency which the families he worked with found it hard to comprehend. But the local council, like many councils across the land, is focused on operating as a business, rather than the public service that so many of its most vulnerable residents rely on.

But he stills goes out, into people's homes, still hooks up with the boys who are caught up in some road madness. He still believes that there is nothing more important than that one conversation or small deed that might just make that difference to stop another Anton dying, another friend grieving and another mother crying. He is still as gullible and just as blind to the motivations of some, praying that he can find the speck of goodness that he can hook into and make that difference. Success and failure will come in many colours.

As all the characters move on, making their own significant changes in their individualistic worlds, so Peckham moves on. She is still changing, still surviving. The colours and vibrancy are coming back. The station is getting a face lift and the shops are slowly changing - still not fast enough for some - but Peckham has generations of time. The front line is not as busy these days, so for the time being she can take a deep breath and enjoy a few quiet moments out of the spotlight.

As a place Peckham will always be gritty and edgy, somewhere that you can feel the pulsation of life. But that is what makes her so special and its community is responding.

Slowly and quietly they talk about their pride of coming from Peckham.

The Experts

Simon Harding
Senior Lecturer, Middlesex University

We are familiar with the many names used to describe these areas - the Streets, the Street World, Gangland, Sink Estates; and the lives of those who live there - Road Life, Real-life, Ghetto Life, Pond Life and worse – but amongst this rash of names and our rush to judgement, we forget it is really about one thing – communities.

Life in our poorer communities has already been condemned, stereotyped and ridiculed by the media. The popular roles have already been cast – neglectful parents, yobbish young people, provocative policing and all this played against a backdrop of violence and crime. Those of us who have worked with these marginalised communities know that this is not the full picture and not the whole story. In fact it is often a media creation. These communities have real people with real feelings and real life challenges. Those living there also laugh, love and bleed. They too have life stories and these stories have value. Only that all too often we devalue their accounts and discount their views. Thus, their voices do not get heard. Their words do not count. They do not register.

Any researcher working in these environments will vouch for the challenges faced daily by such communities. They will no doubt also vouch for the challenges faced in conducting research within these communities. The difficulty of accessing the right people; of showing and gaining respect and building trust – all before a story is told or shared – especially one that might never before have been spoken.

Jonathon's background and work experience has over the years provided him with the opportunity to access this world in all its colour. When presented with this opportunity he did not just touch the sides of this world but immersed himself in it, meeting gang-affiliated young men and women, their mothers, their families, their teachers, their guardians. Overtime, he resolved to hear their stories and to find a way to air them and communicate them to others, so that their stories would not be lost.

This work is therefore undertaken in the best tradition of ethnography: a deep immersion in this world and desire to foreground the voices of those who live in it.

It has no pretensions to situate the work in gang theory. It simply does not need to. In fact, to do so would dampen the raw emotion so evocatively captured and render the experiences no more than a case study. Jonathon has avoided this trap, retaining the integrity of his subjects through his ethnographic approach. The craft of the book is to bring it all together; to build a narrative of the street; to convey feeling, depth and purpose; to evoke, to resonate, to resound.

We owe it therefore to the subjects to offer our time, to hear their story, and as we so seldom do, to take the time ..... to listen.

Silent Voices

Sheldon Thomas
Former gang leader and Gangs Consultant at Gangsline

A very insightful approach with each chapter making for compelling read, giving us the reader a unique insight into gang lifestyle seen from different prospective with individuals who knew and lived with Sunday and carefully placed together. Sunday's life was definitely cut short and whether we the reader wants to indulge with the notion about him and his peeps were just friends, the real reality as always are the deaths of many young men in many inner city estates, not just in London but in areas such as Birmingham, Manchester, Liverpool, Manchester, Luton and Nottingham.

Some researchers often use poverty, unemployment, deprivation as the core reasons why some turn to gangs and crime. The Fabian Society have in my opinion come very close by describing these deprived housing estates as social concentration camps, whilst these may all contribute to the out of control lives style of many young people caught up in gangs, having lived this, Gangsline have found through our own research that gang mentality is not often mentioned and neither is the real issues for most of these young people, especially the boys, their lives are often marred by absent fathers, lack of emotional attachment, rejection, anger, hurt, disillusionment, lies, emotional trauma, fear, insecurity, loneliness and personality disorder and in some communities mental issues is still a stigma, if you compound these issue in close proximity of estate life and with other young people experiencing the same pain going through the same issues mentally and add lack of hope, then you have the formation of gangs in a fractured society.

I have known Jonathon for over 10 years and his understanding of gang culture is unlike most professionals who claim to know about gangs, Jonathon chose to get his hand and feet muddy and even though that sounds like a cliché, Jonathon did not just oversee a team he went out and engaged with some of the most hardcore individuals involved in this lifestyle. This gave Jonathon real credibility and he has given most of his professional life in trying to help those whose lives are often a thin line between life and death.

This book must be read if you want to have some understanding on gangs.

Commander John Sutherland
Metropolitan Police Service

I have worked as a police officer in Inner London since 1992. Since that time, I have stood at too many murder scenes - in the haunted places where young men have lost their lives. It seems to me that violence involving young people has become one of the most pressing issues of our time. And there are no swift or easy answers.

Jonathon Toy understands this - and has dedicated much of his professional life to working with perpetrators, victims and their families.

Before we can begin to resolve the problems we're faced with, we need to have a better conversation about youth violence - starting with the development of a much a better understanding of what it is that we're faced with. This book is an important contribution to that conversation

About the Author

Jonathon Toy is an Expert in the field of community safety for over 16 years. He led an operational team for the Hackney Council working closely with the police to disrupt local drugs markets.

His specialist knowledge in working with young people and families, and developing innovative programmes to address violent crime and gang related violence. Jonathon worked with the Home Office in 2011 following the Summer Riots, advising on programmes to address gang and weapon violence and in the drafting of the "Ending Gang and Youth Violence Report".

Jonathon has published a number of articles and papers on gangs and serious youth violence, most notably a practitioner report in 2009 titled "Die another Day", articles for Safer Communities (Pier Professional Ltd). More recently he was the Head of Community Safety for the London Borough of Lambeth and subsequently Southwark for over 10 years.

Jonathon is a member of the governments national Ending Gang and Youth Violence Team and has served as a Vice Chair the London Heads of Community Safety Group. He now runs his own consultancy company Jonathon Toy Associates, working with statutory and voluntary organisations in the development of intervention programmes to address violence and exploitation.